THE CIVIL WAR QUIZ BOOK

THE

JOHN MALONE

QUILL/WILLIAM MORROW/NEW YORK

It is the policy of William Morrow and Company, Inc., and its imprints and affiliates, recognizing the importance of preserving what has been written, to print the books we publish on acid-free paper, and we exert our best efforts to that end.

Library of Congress Cataloging-in-Publication Data

Malone, John Williams.
    The Civil War quiz book / John Malone.
        p.   cm.
    ISBN 0-688-11269-2
    1. United States—History—Civil War, 1861–1865—Miscellanea.
I. Title.
E468.M19   1992
973—dc20   91-38451   CIP

Printed in the United States of America

First Quill Edition

1 2 3 4 5 6 7 8 9 10

BOOK DESIGN BY LISA STOKES

*This book is for my great-grandfather,
"The Major,"
who told the stories he knew to his grandson,
my father, Miles S. Malone,
who went on to learn a great deal on his own,
and passed it down to me,
and thousands of grateful students.*

Contents

Part One
Prologue to War

Q. When did the issues concerning states' rights and slavery first cause constitutional problems?

A. *During the original drafting of the Constitution in 1787. Southern states were adamant that there be a clause stating that the federal government would ensure the return of fugitive slaves to their owners. Slaves were also counted as three fifths of a person in apportioning the number of congressional representatives. The Southern states did agree to cut off the slave trade with Africa in ten years' time.*

Q. Delegates to a secret convention from what part of the country considered the idea of seceding from the Union in 1814?

A. *This notion was first proposed by New Englanders who were against the War of 1812, which was still going on, although in its final stages.*

Q. Name the two states involved in the Missouri Compromise of 1820.

A. *Missouri and Maine. The House of Representatives voted to admit Maine to the Union. Since Maine would be a "free" state without slaves, Southern politicians raised a ruckus, insisting upon the simultaneous admission of Missouri as a slave state. There were already eleven slave and eleven free states, and the South wanted that balance to continue.*

Q. What was the significance of the latitude reading 36° 30'?

A. *As part of the Missouri Compromise, those parts of the Louisiana Territory north of this line would not be permitted to have slaves. Since the land in what would become such states as Nebraska, the Dakotas, Colorado, and Wyoming was hardly suited to slave crops such as cotton and tobacco, the South went along with this—but Kansas would become a major bone of contention.*

Q. What was the doctrine of nullification and who developed it?

A. *Senator John C. Calhoun of South Carolina developed this doctrine, which held that a state had the right to nullify any federal law it found in violation of the compact that had existed at the time of that state's entry into the Union. It was only a small leap from the theory of nullification to the concept of secession.*

Q. On January 1, 1831, the Bostonian abolitionist William Lloyd Garrison printed on a handpress the first issue of a newspaper that would have great influence in the North and cause outrage in the South. What was the newspaper called?

A. The Liberator, *an extremely outspoken anti-slavery paper, which Garrison published unrelentingly until 1866.*

Q. Name the slave who led a bloody uprising in Virginia in August of 1831.

Prologue to War

A. *Nat Turner, who was caught and executed after he and his followers killed about sixty whites, the majority of them women and children. This uprising led to a two-week debate in the Virginia legislature in January of 1832 on the question of slavery. There was considerable recognition that slavery had an injurious effect on the character of whites and that it was not working well as an economic system. There was even talk of freeing and deporting slaves, but no practical way of doing so could be devised. In the long run, this debate only strengthened the hand of the apologists for slavery.*

Q. In November of 1832, using the reasoning of Calhoun, South Carolina held a state convention that voted to nullify the Federal Tariff Acts of 1828 and 1832, which were widely regarded in the South as discriminatory against the region. Was there any talk of secession at this time?

A. *Yes, causing President Andrew Jackson to issue a warning against it. A major crisis was averted when "the Great Pacificator," Henry Clay, pushed a new compromise tariff bill through Congress.*

Q. When Texas gained its independence from Mexico in April of 1836, it quickly asked that it either be annexed by the United States or be recognized as an independent republic. Why was annexation a very sticky political problem?

A. *Texas had fought for its independence in large part because Mexico had outlawed slavery, and it was determined to preserve the institution. President Jackson finally recognized Texas as a republic on his last day in office in March of 1837.*

Q. In 1838 a Maryland slave named Frederick Augustus Washington Bailey, whose mistress had taught him to read and write, escaped to freedom. What did he change his name to?

A. *Frederick Douglass. Just twenty-one when he escaped, Douglass went on to become one of the most eloquent and influential abolitionist voices. During the Civil War itself, he played a very important role in raising black regiments.*

Q. In April of 1844, President John Tyler, who had succeeded William Henry Harrison after his death from pneumonia in 1841, signed a treaty of annexation with Texas. What was the Senate's response?

A. *It voted against it, trying to avoid further conflict between the free and slave states.*

Q. In the 1844 presidential election, what was the most clearly drawn issue between the Democratic winner James Polk and the Whig loser Henry Clay?

A. *Polk was an expansionist, who wanted to bring not only Texas but also California and Oregon into the Union. Clay had made clear he was against the annexation of Texas.*

Q. Polk proved his expansionist credentials by provoking a war with Mexico. In August of 1846, three months into the war, Polk requested that Congress appropriate $2 million to acquire land from Mexico once the war was over. Who was David Wilmot and what was the spanner he threw into the works?

A. *Wilmot, a Democratic representative from Pennsylvania, only in his first term, tried to add a proviso to the appropriations bill that would have banned not only slavery but any "involuntary servitude" in lands acquired from Mexico. The House passed the Wilmot Proviso but the Senate did not and it was omitted from the final bill. But it stirred up a terrific storm, adding to the growing tensions between North and South. Wilmot eventually became a Republican, wrote that party's platform in 1856, and was temporary chairman of the convention that nominated Lincoln.*

Q. The Treaty of Guadalupe Hidalgo gave Texas to the United States, as well as land that would ultimately form the whole of or part of how many states?

A. *Seven states, including all of California, Nevada, and Utah, large sections of New Mexico and Arizona, and parts of Colorado and Wyoming. Curiously, Polk regarded the ceded territory as "inadequate," as did many Southern politicians. But it was more than large enough to cause intense and bitter debate about how it should be organized and whether it should be open to slavery or not.*

Q. During the Mexican War, the Polk administration had tried to sabotage General Zachary Taylor, a Whig whose star was rising fast, by withholding reinforcements, but Taylor still prevailed against a force four times the size of his own and became a national hero. His exploits gained him the presidency in 1848 against Democratic candidate Lewis Cass. Did Taylor overwhelm the Democratic candidate?

A. *Far from it. Although Cass is little remembered, he was a very important figure of his era, and he received more electoral votes than any losing candidate in American history up to that time—127 to Taylor's 163—a record that would stand for twenty years. In the popular vote he lost by 184,533 votes out of 2,580,645 cast. Cass had served as the civil governor of Michigan and brought it into statehood. He was secretary of war from 1831 to 1836, subsequently served as the ambassador to France, held a Senate seat from 1845 to 1857, and was secretary of state from 1857 to 1860. In terms of the slavery issue, he was the originator of an idea that came to be called "popular sovereignty." This concept attempted to get around the slavery problem by leaving the question up to each territory. It would play a major role in the turbulent 1850s.*

Q. In December of 1849, President Taylor requested Congress to admit California as a state. It would be a free state, upsetting the balance so dear to Southerners, and causing John Calhoun to bring up secession again. What was Taylor's answer to that?

A. *The former general said he would put down any attempt at secession if he had to personally lead the troops. Taylor was in fact a slave owner himself, but not at all sympathetic with extreme Southern positions on the subject.*

Q. On January 29, 1850, the now seventy-three-year-old Senator Henry Clay outlined a plan to put the slavery issue to rest. The always practical Clay sought to balance the interests of North and South. California would be admitted as a free state—but the fugitive-slave laws would be strengthened. The slave trade would be abolished in Washington, D.C.—but interstate trading in slaves would not otherwise be interfered with. And the popular-sovereignty ideas of Lewis Cass would be applied to the new territories. The South was not happy with this plan. It was imperative, as Southerners saw it, to open up new areas to slavery in order to more widely disperse the constantly increasing slave population, in order to avoid much larger and more dangerous repeats of Nat Turner's rebellion. Did or did not John C. Calhoun make an impassioned speech against the compromise?

A. *He wrote the speech but, only weeks from his death, was too ill to deliver it. Senator James M. Mason of Virginia gave it for him. This speech was countered on March 7 by the great orator from Massachusetts, Daniel Webster, who was against slavery morally, but who above all wanted to preserve the Union. Still, the Senate was deadlocked. Then fate intervened. President Taylor, who was against the compromise and had totally broken with Clay over the issue, suddenly died on July 9. Millard Fillmore, who supported the compromise, became president, and Senator Stephen Douglas broke up Clay's package and shepherded the components through Congress one at a time.*

Q. In June of 1851 a serialized novel began to appear in an abolitionist journal called *The National Era*. It was published in book form the following year. Harriet Beecher Stowe's *Uncle Tom's Cabin* ripped through the fabric of the Compromise of 1850 even before political events inevitably shredded it for good. How many copies of Mrs. Stowe's novel were sold between its publication and the outbreak of the Civil War?

A. *It sold what was for that time a staggering one million copies. Perhaps even more important, countless stage versions of the book were mounted, and audiences were able to cheer Eliza crossing the ice, weep at the plight of Uncle Tom, and hiss the evil Simon Legree, the plantation manager whom Mrs. Stowe had very cleverly made a transplanted Yankee. Abolitionist fever began to rise again in the North.*

Q. Before the fever really rose, however, Franklin Pierce, a relatively obscure New Hampshire politician with few enemies, was nominated by the Democrats on the forty-ninth ballot and went on to defeat the other hero of the Mexican War, General Winfield Scott. Next to other Democratic figures like Lewis Cass, James Buchanan (who had been Polk's secretary of state), and the young firebrand from Illinois, Stephen A. Douglas, Pierce was a virtual mosquito. Why did he win?

A. *He was handsome, charming, and supported the Compromise of 1850 very strongly. To a nation trying desperately to pretend that nothing was so wrong that it couldn't be papered over, Franklin Pierce was the perfect head-in-the-sand candidate.*

Q. Pierce got through two fairly uneventful years before Senator Douglas, ''the little giant,'' tore all the old wounds open with an astonishing proposal that two new territorial governments be formed, one to be called Kansas and the other Nebraska, with the people of the territories left to decide on the slavery issue according to the popular-sovereignty ideas of Lewis Cass. Why did this proposal cause such an uproar in 1854?

A. *Because both states were above the 36° 30' line that had been established with the Missouri Compromise. Douglas opened a Pandora's box with this proposal. Douglas was a great politician, and he got his bill through Congress and signed by a supportive President Pierce, who despite his New England heritage was no friend of the abolitionists. A practical glad-handing politician, he regarded the abolitionists as moralistic extremists.*

Q. One consequence of Douglas's proposal was the foundation of Emigrant Aid Societies. What did these do?

A. *They provided assistance to any family that would move to the new territories and vote against making that territory a potential slave state.*

Prologue to War

Q. What new party was created in July of 1854?

A. *The Republican party was born in Jackson, Michigan, as a convention met to oppose the Kansas-Nebraska Act. The party was initially composed of fairly diverse elements, including members of the small but influential Free-Soil party that had sprung up six years earlier, Northern Whigs, and even Northern Democrats who felt the time had come to call a halt to the expansion of slavery.*

Q. With the birth of the Republican party and the defection of many Southern Whigs to the Democratic party because of Stephen Douglas's position on territories, the Whig party virtually collapsed. Some members went over to the Republican party, but others joined another new political group called the American party. What was the curious nickname of the American party?

A. *It was called the Know-Nothing party because it kept both its organization and its membership secret. It had considerable success in the North in the elections of 1854, but its strongly anti-Catholic views, together with its vagueness on many other issues, caused it to fall apart within three years.*

Q. Why did thousands of Missourians cross the border into Kansas in March of 1885?

A. *Elections were being held in Kansas for a territorial legislature, and the pro-slavery Missourians were able to swing the vote sufficiently to elect a pro-slavery legislature. Outraged anti-slavery Kansans held a convention in the fall, elected an anti-slavery legislature, and passed a constitution banning slavery. The territory was now in chaos.*

Q. Lawrence, Kansas, named for a wealthy Massachusetts man, Amos A. Lawrence, who had founded an Emigration Aid

Society, was the home of two anti-slavery newspapers, the *Kansas Free State* and the *Herald of Freedom*. What happened to this town on March 21, 1856?

A. *It was attacked by a posse of nearly a thousand pro-slavery men, who destroyed the newspaper printing shops, set fire to the Free State Hotel, and sacked several private homes. The new territory soon became known as "Bleeding Kansas," and a small-scale civil war ensued in the territory.*

Q. In 1856 the Republican party, only two years after its founding, nominated as presidential candidate the famous western explorer John C. Frémont. How well did he do against the Democratic candidate, James Buchanan of Pennsylvania?

A. *Considering how new the party was, Frémont did remarkably well, amassing 1,391,555 votes to Buchanan's 1,927,995.*

Q. In March of 1857, the Supreme Court handed down its decision concerning the status of Dred Scott, the slave of an army doctor who had taken Scott with him to Illinois and then to the Wisconsin Territory. He was then taken back to Missouri, where a case was brought that because Scott had resided in a free state and a free territory, he should now be considered a freeman. The Supreme Court went far beyond settling this issue, however. The majority held that not only was Scott still a slave but that the Missouri Compromise was unconstitutional—Congress did not have the authority to ban slavery in a territory. Three of the judges, including Chief Justice Roger Taney, who had held that position since 1836, went so far as to say that no black man could become a citizen of the United States even if he were free, and thus had no right to redress in the courts. Did any members of the Court hold that Dred Scott was a freeman?

A. *Yes, Justices John McLean of Ohio and Benjamin Curtis of Massachusetts. Curtis's dissent was particularly strong. But the damage was done and feelings about the issue of slavery were greatly intensified.*

Q. On what occasion did the former one-term congressman from Illinois, Abraham Lincoln, say, "A house divided against itself cannot stand. I believe this government cannot endure half slave and half free"?

A. *In his speech accepting the nomination of the Illinois Republican party to run against the incumbent Senator Stephen A. Douglas in the 1858 elections. The ensuing debates against Douglas at towns and cities throughout the state did a great deal for Lincoln's reputation. He more than held his own against Douglas, who was regarded as one of the great orators of the time, and even though he lost a close election, his name was now known throughout the United States.*

Q. In October of 1859, the voters of Kansas went to the polls to do what that Congress had demanded?

A. *To vote yet again on a territorial constitution. Twice before a bill that would have admitted Kansas to the Union under a slave-state constitution had been defeated. This time, without outside interference, Kansas voted to ratify an anti-slavery constitution.*

Q. On the night of October 16, 1859, the fanatical abolitionist John Brown, who already had numerous bloody deeds behind him, launched a raid on the federal arsenal at Harpers Ferry, Virginia. Although he had only eighteen men with him, including three of his sons and five free blacks, his plan was to lead a slave uprising. But the slaves he had expected to flock to his side did not appear, and two days later he and his followers were cornered in a railroad engine-house. Name the Virginia colonel who led the militia that captured Brown.

A. *He was Colonel Robert E. Lee. Two of Brown's sons were killed during the capture and Brown himself was wounded. He was hastily tried and convicted of three capital crimes: treason, murder, and inciting a slave insurrection. He made a memorable speech at the end of the trial and in the North there was great sympathy for him. Although there were certainly grounds for the governor of Virginia to commute his sentence because of insanity, he was hanged on December 2 and immediately achieved the status of a martyr.*

Q. Why did the Southern delegates to the Democratic Convention in Charleston, South Carolina, walk out in April of 1860?

A. *Because Stephen A. Douglas, the obvious candidate, refused to accept Jefferson Davis's plank in the platform calling for all territories to be opened to slavery—which was completely at odds with the popular-sovereignty concept Douglas held. The convention eventually disbanded in confusion, and was reconvened in Baltimore in June. Again the Southerners walked out, but Douglas was nominated. The Southern Democrats then met to nominate their own candidate, Vice-President John C. Breckinridge.*

Q. At the Republican convention in Chicago in May it seemed at first that Governor William E. Seward of New York would be quickly nominated. But he had many enemies in the party, and secondary candidates like Edward Bates of Missouri, Salmon P. Chase of Ohio, and Simon Cameron of Pennsylvania were determined to stop him. Abraham Lincoln seemed an obvious choice because of his famous debates against the likely Democratic candidate Douglas (the second Democratic convention would not be held until the following month). On what ballot was Lincoln nominated?

A. *On the second ballot, Lincoln built up momentum, and on the third, one block of votes after another switched to him, putting him over the top.*

Q. In November Lincoln was elected with a clear majority of the electoral vote. Did he also achieve a majority in the popular vote?

A. *No. With three other candidates in the field—Douglas, Breckinridge, and John Bell of the Constitutional Union party—Lincoln commanded only a plurality. But the Democratic hope that no one would get an electoral majority, thus throwing the election into the House of Representatives, did not materialize. Abraham Lincoln was the new president, only six years after the formation of his party.*

Q. During the election campaign Lincoln had made it clear that he was not going to tamper with slavery in the existing slave states. But he was uncompromising on the question of the territories: Slavery would not be extended to them. That in itself was too much for the South. The first Southern state voted to secede in December. Which state was it?

A. *South Carolina, always the most militant state on the subject of slavery. The Union began to dissolve.*

Q. In 1860, how many of the nation's firearms were manufactured in Northern states that would join the Union cause?

  a. More than 80 percent
  b. More than 90 percent
  c. Close to 100 percent

A. *The answer is c, the figure put at 97 percent. This was one reason why many believed the South could not possibly decide to enter into armed conflict.*

Part Two
1861

Q. Following the lead of South Carolina, six more Southern states seceded from the Union early in 1861: Mississippi on January 9, Florida on January 10, Alabama on the eleventh, Georgia on the nineteenth, Louisiana on the twenty-sixth, and Texas on February 1. In all six cases the vote was taken by the state legislature. Which state had the largest margin for secession and which had the smallest?

A. *The largest margin was in Texas, which voted 106 to 7 for secession; the smallest was in Georgia, where the vote was 208 to 89, indicating the considerable Union support in that state.*

Q. On January 21, what action did Jefferson Davis and five other Southern senators take on the floor of the Senate?

A. *Withdrawing from the Senate, all six gave farewell speeches.*

Q. In the first ten days of 1861, numerous Federal forts and arsenals were seized by state militias in South Carolina, Georgia, Florida, and Louisiana, including Fort Pulaski in Georgia and the important arsenal at Baton Rouge, Louisiana. How much resistance did these actions arouse?

A. *Virtually none. Most of the forts and arsenals were un-manned.*

Q. This fort in the mouth of Charleston Bay was located on an artificial island. It had taken ten years to build at a cost of half a million dollars. Name it.

A. *Fort Sumter. This fort and Fort Pickens on Santa Rosa Island off the coast of Florida were both manned by Federal troops, adding to their strategic importance.*

Q. On January 5, the merchant ship *Star of the West* was dispatched from New York with 250 Federal troops aboard to bolster the garrison at Fort Sumter. Why wasn't a commissioned naval vessel employed for this purpose?

A. *A merchant ship was felt to be less provocative. In addition, if it was fired upon, war would not be the inevitable result, as would have been the case with an official navy ship. It was in fact fired upon as it approached Fort Sumter, and quickly retreated.*

Q. Despite President Buchanan's policy of avoiding direct confrontation with Southern states, he did order that Fort Taylor, at Key West, Florida, be garrisoned by Federal troops on January 14. Why did this prove to be a crucial decision?

A. *Its strategic position was to provide a vital Gulf Coast base for the Union throughout the war.*

Q. On February 4, former President John Tyler opened the Peace Convention in Washington, D.C.; the object of the

131 representatives from twenty-two states was to find a compromise that would preserve the Union. What other group began deliberations in Montgomery, Alabama, on the same date?

A. *The Provisional Congress of the Confederate States.*

Q. Congressional approval was given for the entry of the thirty-fourth state into the Union on January 29. Name this "border" state.

A. *Kansas, which had finally adopted a constitution that outlawed slavery.*

Q. For what high position were Robert Toombs, Howell Cobb, Robert Rhett, Alexander Stephens, and William Yancey considered in February of 1861?

A. *President of the Confederate States. Rhett and Yancey were regarded as too extreme; Cobb was felt to have supported the Union too long. Many believed that Toombs had the greatest ability and would have been fit for the job, but he was passed over for Jefferson Davis, who had offended no one and whose moderation was felt important in wooing the border states. Stephens was voted vice-president. Both he and Davis were confirmed unanimously.*

Q. Jefferson Davis was named president of the Confederate States on February 9. He was not in Montgomery but at home on his plantation in Mississippi. When a telegram arrived the next day from the Provisional Congress to inform him of his election, he was both surprised and somewhat disappointed. Why was he disappointed?

A. He had served with distinction in the Mexican War and as secretary of war under President Franklin Pierce. His hope had been to be named General-in-Chief of the Confederate Army.

Q. What was Jefferson Davis's seldom used middle name?

A. Finis.

Q. On February 11, two men left their hometowns in two different states on equally fateful journeys. Who were they?

A. Jefferson Davis left his plantation, Brierfield, for Montgomery to be sworn in as president of the Confederate States. President-elect Abraham Lincoln departed from his home in Springfield, Illinois, for the journey to Washington for his inauguration on March 4.

Q. What tune was for the first time scored for performance by a band, to accompany the inaugural ride of Jefferson Davis on February 18?

A. "Dixie."

Q. On Washington's Birthday, Lincoln, continuing his journey toward Washington, gave a speech in Philadelphia. He was to have continued to the capital through Maryland, but an assassination threat and the large number of Southern sympathizers known to exist in Maryland caused a change in plans. He took a different route, accompanied only by a friend and a man known as America's first detective. Give the last name of the detective.

A. *Pinkerton. Allan Pinkerton would also serve as the first head of General McClellan's secret service.*

Q. On February 28, North Carolina held an election on the question of whether to hold a state convention to debate secession. Union sympathizers defeated the call for a convention by how many votes?

    a. 2,000
    b. 700
    c. fewer than 200

A. *The call was defeated by fewer than 200 votes—46,603 to 46,409.*

Q. When Lincoln said, in his inaugural address on March 4, ". . . in *your* hands, my dissatisfied fellow countrymen, and not in *mine,* is the momentous issue of civil war," was he chastising the South about the institution of slavery?

A. *No. He emphasized, as he had all along, that he was not against slavery where it already existed but opposed to its spread to other territories and yet-to-be-admitted states.*

Q. Why, in the weeks after his inauguration, did Lincoln oppose any meetings between members of his government and envoys from the Southern states?

A. *He didn't want to recognize the Confederacy in any way, thus temporarily sidestepping the issue of whether or not the Confederate States had actually left the Union.*

Q. In late February and early March, the new Republican House and Senate passed, by the necessary two-thirds majority, a constitutional amendment. Called the Corwin Amendment after the Ohio congressman who presented it, it would have become the Thirteenth Amendment if it had been ratified by the states. It was, in fact, precisely the opposite in its intent from the actual Thirteenth Amendment, passed in 1865. What did the Corwin Amendment say?

A. *It stated that the Constitution should never be altered to interfere with the institutions of the states, including the institution of slavery. The Corwin Amendment was thus a last-ditch attempt to placate the South. But it came too late and was ignored. The Confederacy was already involved in writing its own constitution.*

Q. The "permanent" Constitution of the Confederate States was passed on March 11. It adhered closely to the U.S. Constitution, including the Bill of Rights. It did guarantee the right of slavery in the territories, but to the surprise of the North, it outlawed international slave trading. It attempted to make some practical improvements as well. One of these gave to the president an economic power that in our own time both President Reagan and President Bush have called for a constitutional amendment to provide. What was this economic power?

A. *The line-item veto. The Confederate Constitution also set the term of president at six years—another idea that has achieved much currency in our own time.*

Q. At the beginning of April, Lincoln decided to send relief forces to both Fort Sumter and Fort Pickens in Florida. He wrote to Major Robert A. Anderson, the commander at Fort Sumter, telling him to maintain the situation as it existed but giving him the right to choose a course of action should hostilities develop. Three days later, General Pierre Gustave Toutant Beauregard, in command of the Confederate forces at Charleston, sent Major Anderson a message stating that further contact between the fort and Charleston was forbidden. General Beauregard and Major Anderson knew one another well. What was their relationship?

A. *A decade earlier, Major Anderson had been one of the prize pupils of General Beauregard, then an artillery instructor at West Point. Beauregard had served as the commander of West Point for the first few weeks in 1861, resigning to take charge of the Confederate forces in Charleston.*

Q. On the eleventh of April, General Beauregard demanded, through envoys, that Major Anderson evacuate Fort Sumter. Anderson refused. A second request the following day was countered by an offer to evacuate on the fifteenth if Anderson had received no further orders from Washington. Why was this unacceptable to the Confederacy?

A. *They were certain relief forces from the North must be in transit.*

Q. After refusing to accept Anderson's delay, how long did the Confederate forces give him to evacuate before an attack began?

    a.   24 hours
    b.   6 hours
    c.   1 hour

A. *1 hour.*

The Civil War Quiz Book

Q. The Charleston Harbor batteries began a bombardment of Fort Sumter that lasted through the day and a good part of the night. Approximately 40,000 shells were fired during the battle. How many combatants were killed?

A. *None, and there were few injuries on either side. Even so, Major Anderson decided that he had too few supplies and men to hold on, and surrendered. The Union ships that had been sent to relieve the fort could be seen at sea, but did not engage.*

Q. Even as the bombardment of Fort Sumter was taking place, the Union navy secured an ultimately more important prize. Name it.

A. *The forces sent to relieve Fort Pickens on Santa Rosa Island off the Florida coast landed successfully, a loss that would haunt the Confederacy during the subsequent embargo of Southern harbors.*

Q. Is there any comparison between Lincoln's handling of the situation at Fort Sumter and President Franklin Delano Roosevelt's handling of Pearl Harbor in 1941?

A. *Yes. There have long been charges that Roosevelt had been warned of the Pearl Harbor attack, but let it proceed because he felt that that was the only way to get a still-isolationist America into World War II. Similarly, there have been those who have accused Lincoln of purposefully bungling the relief of Fort Sumter in order to ensure that the South would be the first to fire and could thus be accused of starting the war. The evidence against both Roosevelt and Lincoln is circumstantial but suspicious.*

Q. Northerners held that the bombardment of Fort Sumter was the start of the war. Southerners held that it began with the call-up of 75,000 militia by Lincoln on April 15, 1861, and the institution of the embargo against the South on April 27. The Supreme Court was eventually called on to settle the question. How did it vote?

A. *In a 5 to 4 decision, the Court held that the war began at Fort Sumter. The other four justices took a different approach, stating that it began on July 31, when the Confederacy declared a state of war.*

Q. As war broke out, the difference in size of the populations of the Union and Confederate States seemed to put the South at a great disadvantage. The Union population was 22 million. The Confederate population was 9 million. Of that Confederate population, how many were slaves?

    a. 2.5 million
    b. 3.5 million
    c. 3.8 million

A. *There were 3.5 million slaves.*

Q. The discrepancies in population meant that the North's potential pool of soldiers was four times as large as the South's. Ultimately, though, the Southern population was more committed. What was the ratio of Southerners who fought in the war as compared to Northerners?

A. *Two to one.*

Q. At the beginning of 1861, there were 16,000 men in the regular U.S. Army and Navy. How many of these men defected to the Confederate forces?

A. *3,000 men.*

Q. In terms of West Point graduates, what was the split between those who fought for the Union and those who fought for the Confederacy?
   a. More fought for the North.
   b. The split was even.
   c. More fought for the South.

A. *More West Point graduates fought for the South. The South had far more military schools that prepared boys for West Point as well as a much greater interest in military matters. It was because so many of the finest of West Point's graduates fought for the South that, especially in the early years of the war, the Confederate forces were able to do so well. They were often better led.*

Q. How many of Mary Todd Lincoln's three sisters were married to Confederate officers?

A. *All three were married to Confederate officers. One brother was also a Confederate officer and another a Confederate physician in the field. But her favorite brother, Robert, was a Union officer. There were always whispers in Washington about Mary Todd Lincoln's loyalty, but these were in fact unfair. Her loyalty to her husband was absolute, even obsessional, and since most of her family had disparaged her rawboned husband, Mrs. Lincoln was hardly disposed to care what they thought or did.*

Q. What was the response of the state of Virginia to Lincoln's call for 75,000 militia to put down the insurrection in South Carolina?

A. *The Virginia State Convention reversed the earlier vote of the legislature and called for secession, with a referendum to be held May 23.*

Q. What post did Lincoln, through emissaries, offer to Robert E. Lee on April 19?

A. *Commander of the Union forces. Lee resigned his post with the Federal army the following day.*

Q. Also on the nineteenth, Lincoln ordered that all Southern ports be blockaded. In response, Jefferson Davis declared that the Confederacy would accept applications for letters of marque, in order to facilitate privateering. In the North what was privateering regarded as being?

A. *Piracy on the seas.*

Q. Further indication of war fever was demonstrated on the nineteenth when the 6th Massachusetts Regiment, on its way to Washington, was attacked in Baltimore by pro-South rioters, resulting in casualties on both sides. These events inspired the composition of a famous song which begins with the words "The despot's heel is on thy shore." Name the song.

A. *"Maryland, My Maryland."*

Q. Like Maryland, Missouri was a very unsettled state with many sympathizers on both sides. On April 25, Captain James H. Stokes of Chicago made a daring secret raid across the border from Alton, Illinois, with a small group of men to

St. Louis. What did he return to Illinois with the following day?

A. *Ten thousand muskets taken from the Federal arsenal in St. Louis.*

Q. Also on the twenty-fifth, the 7th New York Regiment arrived in Washington to the great relief of Lincoln, who was deeply concerned that the continuing unrest in Maryland would lead to an attack on the capital. On the twenty-ninth, the Maryland legislature presented Lincoln with an even greater cause for relief. What was it?

A. *The Maryland legislature voted 53 to 13 against secession. Although there was some slavery in the state and much sympathy toward the South, Maryland's economy was much more closely bound to the North than the South. Sheer practicality demanded a vote for the Union.*

Q. On May 3, Lincoln called for 42,000 volunteer soldiers and 18,000 seamen. This was followed three days later by secessionist votes in two contiguous states. Name them.

A. *The Arkansas legislature voted 69 to 1 for secession; in Tennessee the vote was 66 to 25, but because of considerable division in the state a public referendum on the issue was also set.*

Q. In early May Lincoln named a Union officer who had achieved national recognition the previous month to recruit soldiers in Kentucky and West Virginia. Who was this officer?

A. *Major Anderson, whose actions at Fort Sumter were regarded as a fine combination of bravery and sound judgment.*

Q. At the same time, the U.S.S. *Constitution* and the steamer *Baltic* made anchor at Newport, R.I., as part of the transfer of the functions of a famous military institution from another state. Name the institution.

A. *Annapolis. It was felt that the situation in Maryland was still sufficiently volatile that the Naval Academy should be relocated in a securely Union state.*

Q. What did Queen Victoria announce on May 13?

A. *The neutrality of Great Britain.*

Q. Great Britain's neutrality was a serious setback for the Confederacy. It had been their view and hope, in what was called Cotton Diplomacy, that the need for cotton by British mills would lead England to side with the South. But England had a glut of cotton at the time and was also beginning to import it from India and other colonies. Beyond that, the North had practiced another kind of diplomacy. What was it called?

A. *Wheat Diplomacy. The importation of wheat from the Northern states was if anything of greater importance to England than cotton.*

Q. On May 20, a state whose legislature had earlier voted narrowly against secession now voted for it at a state assembly. Name the state.

A. *North Carolina.*

Q. On the same date the Confederate Provisional Congress voted to transfer the capital of the Confederacy from Montgomery, Alabama, to another Southern capital. Name it.

A. Richmond, Virginia.

Q. The May 23 referendum in Virginia produced a vote of 97,000 for secession and 32,000 against. Why was this vote in many ways misleading?

A. The western part of the state was strongly against secession and had already begun to talk of splitting away from the rest of the state.

Q. Name the two Gulf ports that were successfully blockaded on May 26 by Union ships.

A. Mobile, Alabama, and New Orleans, Louisiana.

Q. At the end of May a woman regarded as one of the great American humanitarians and reformers offered her services in establishing hospital care for Union soldiers. Less than two weeks later she was put in charge of all Union nurses. Name her.

A. Dorothea Dix, a wealthy Bostonian, who had devoted the previous two decades to the reform of prisons, poorhouses, and insane asylums.

Q. On June 3 a great rival of Lincoln died. Name him.

A. Stephen A. Douglas. Lincoln led the nation in mourning the man who had defeated him for senator and whom he had defeated for the presidency. Although Douglas apparently died of typhoid, he had been in considerably weakened condition since his unprecedented traveling during the campaign of 1860.

1861

Q. What state ratified secession by a vote of 104,913 to 47,238 on June 8?

A. *Tennessee. It was, however, to remain a hotbed of Union sympathizers throughout the war.*

Q. In mid-June, Lincoln observed a demonstration of an invention of Professor Thaddeus S. C. Lowe. Some believed the invention might be useful in military reconnaissance. What was it?

A. *A hot-air balloon. The Civil War produced more military innovations than any previous conflict in history.*

Q. On June 19, a provisional governor was elected of what would become a new state. Name it.

A. *West Virginia, which thus began the process of separating itself from the Commonwealth and aligning itself with the Union.*

Q. In early July, in Chesapeake Bay, Captain Budd of the steamer *Resolute* noticed something in the water floating toward the U.S.S. *Pawnee*. He retrieved it; subsequent newspaper reports referred to the object as an "infernal machine." What was it?

A. *A sea mine. The Confederates were pioneers in the use of floating mines, at that time called "torpedoes."*

Q. Skirmishes between small forces at Bethel Church, Virginia, and Carthage, Mississippi, on July 5 gave early hope to which side?

A. *The Confederacy.*

Q. On July 11, 12, and 13, forces under the command of thirty-five-year-old General George B. McClellan achieved minor victories at Rich Mountain, Carrick's Ford, and Laurel Hill in western Virginia. Confederate General Robert S. Garnett was killed at Carrick's Ford. For which of the following reason were these victories important?

    a. They helped consolidate the pro-Union sentiments in western Virginia.

    b. They provided bases for deeper forays into Confederate Virginia.

    c. They gave General McClellan a fame out of proportion to the scope of the encounters themselves.

A. *All three consequences were important, but the third had particularly telling early results. The amount of newspaper coverage given to McClellan's exploits put him in a position that allowed him to leapfrog over several more senior generals in the Union chain of command only two weeks later.*

Q. The General-in-Chief of the U.S. Army was seventy-five-year-old Winfield Scott, a hero of the Mexican War but now too fat to mount a horse. He nevertheless had wide respect and was surprised that Lincoln should be resistant to his ideas about how war should be waged against the South. His strategy was to blockade the Southern ports—that was already being done—and then to move down the Mississippi, cutting the South off from the West. Why was this called the Anaconda Plan?

A. *Because, like the action of an anaconda snake, it was intended to strangle the Confederacy to death.*

Q. General Irvin McDowell, Commander of the Army of the Potomac, also favored the Anaconda Plan. But Lincoln, backed by public opinion, had a different strategy. What was it?

A. *To strike aggressively at the heart of the Confederacy through Virginia.*

Q. Following McClellan's victories in western Virginia, General Scott became more enthusiastic about a strike down through Virginia to the new capital of Richmond. In the way stood a force of 22,000 men commanded by the Confederate General P.G.T. Beauregard, who had ordered the bombardment of Fort Sumter. He was located at Manassas, Virginia. From the map on page 44, can you see why Manassas was an almost inevitable point of conflict?

A. *Although located in a sparsely populated area, Manassas was a key railroad junction and stood directly on the route to Richmond.*

Q. General McDowell headed a Union force of 37,000 men as he made his way into Virginia. Beauregard, with only 22,000, sent for the help of his superior, General Joseph Johnston, who was at the head of a smaller force in the Shenandoah Valley, where he was opposed by a larger Union army at Harpers Ferry. Why did General McDowell feel he did not have to worry about Johnston's army?

    a. The Union army at Harpers Ferry was expected to hold him.

    b. It was not believed Johnston could get to Manassas soon enough.

A. *The answer is* a. *But Johnston managed to slip away before dawn.*

Q. How long had the great majority of the soldiers on both sides been in training as the confrontation at Manassas began?

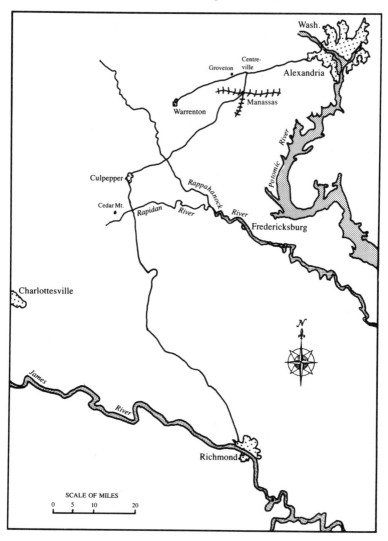

A. *Three months. Most had never been in battle before.*

Q. The battle that followed was the first of two major confrontations on this site. In the South, these two Virginia battles are called to this day First Manassas and Second Manassas.

In the North they are called First Bull Run and Second Bull Run. Why?

A. *Bull Run was a creek at Manassas. The Union forces usually called their battles by the name of the nearest creek or river; the Confederates used the name of the nearest town or junction. Thus many Civil War battles have two names.*

Q. True or false: Manassas was close enough to Washington so that congressmen and Washington society ladies drove out to watch the battle from the surrounding hills on that twenty-first of July.

A. *This is true. Many of the soldiers also took the coming conflict lightly. Governor Andrew of Massachusetts said afterward that many men from his state behaved as though they were going to a town meeting.*

Q. At first, as the battle was joined, it seemed that the Union army would rout the Confederates. Many Southern soldiers abandoned their positions and ran. But as the retreating soldiers reached the steep incline of Henry House Hill, they discovered an entrenched Southern line that was holding fast. This regiment was commanded by a former teacher at the Virginia Military Institute. There, because of many peculiar habits, including sucking incessantly on lemons, he had been called by the nickname "Tom Fool." But as he held his men in line at Henry House Hill, he acquired a new nickname that would be his forever. Who was this general and how did he get his nickname?

A. *Another Confederate commander, retreating with his men, came upon the force on Henry House Hill and called out, "Look! There is Jackson standing like a stone wall! Rally behind the Virginians." Thus did General Thomas J. Jack-*

son, only recently "Tom Fool," become transformed into the legendary "Stonewall Jackson."

Q. Jackson held Henry House Hill and other Confederate troops massed behind him. And then Jackson made a counterattack, urging his men to cry out like the furies as they moved forward. What did this cry quickly come to be called?

A. *The Rebel Yell.*

Q. As the heat of the battle intensified, why was there confusion over which side many soldiers were actually fighting on?

A. *Uniforms had not yet been fully standardized. There were many Union soldiers in gray uniforms and even more Confederate soldiers in blue uniforms.*

Q. There were troops at Manassas dressed in baggy pants, red sashes, balloon-sleeved jackets and red fezlike caps. What did they call themselves?

A. *Zouaves, after the French soldiers in Africa from whom they adopted their costume. There were eventually famous Zouave companies and even regiments from New York City, Chicago, and the state of Indiana.*

Q. There were 1,000 men in a regiment. How many companies were there to a regiment?

A. *Ten.*

Q. The battle of First Bull Run, which at first had seemed an easy Northern victory, had now turned into a seesaw battle raging back and forth over the undulating countryside. The congressmen and their ladies had fled from the hillsides. Great numbers of wounded and dead from both sides were scattered across the fields. It seemed a stalemate, a very bloody one. But then in the distance a fresh regiment appeared. Some of the men were in blue, others in gray. Was it a Union or a Confederate force? Whichever it proved to be would mean victory for one side or the other. The flag of the standard bearer could be seen, but it hung limp in the hot air. Why couldn't they tell which flag it was?

A. *The Confederate flag at that time was so similar to the Federal flag that from a distance it was possible to tell them apart only when they were unfurled in the wind. After First Manassas, the Confederate flag was changed to make it more distinctive, just as a new standardization of uniforms was put in place by both sides (except of course for the Zouaves, who were always Union soldiers).*

Q. At last a breeze lifted the drooping mystery flag. It was Confederate, and the South went on to drive the Union forces from the field of battle. Yet, in fact, this fresh force should not really have been vital to the outcome for either side. Why not?

A. *Of the 37,000 Union troops present at the battle, only 18,000 were actually engaged. Only half the Confederate force of 32,000 was engaged and a third of those, led by Stonewall Jackson's men, did most of the fighting.*

Q. A state convention had been called in Missouri to vote on secession. The Governor, Claiborne F. Jackson, was a virulent secessionist. When the convention adjourned on July 22, was Missouri in the Union or Confederate camp?

A. *Despite Jackson's strong position, the convention sided with the Union. But the question was far from settled. Jackson subsequently responded to Lincoln's call for troops with great invective: "Your requisition is illegal, unconstitutional, revolutionary, inhuman, diabolical, and cannot be complied with."*

Q. General McDowell's failure at First Bull Run made it impossible to retain him as Commander of the Army of the Potomac. With what young general did Lincoln replace him on July 27?

A. *General McClellan, whose minor victories in western Virginia had made him a public favorite.*

Q. The pro-Union leaders in Missouri decided they had had enough of Governor Jackson, and on July 27 took steps to oust him. What did they do?

A. *They declared the offices of governor, lieutenant governor, and several other incumbents open. The next day they elected Hamilton Gamble as governor. In effect, this meant that Missouri had two sets of public officials.*

Q. In early August a monetary bill was passed by Congress that mandated what for the first time in American history?

A. *A national income tax. It called for a levy of 3 percent on income over $800, but was never put into effect.*

Q. On August 5, Rufus King relinquished his post as Lincoln's minister to Rome and returned to America for what purpose?

A. *To take command of a division of Union troops. General King fought at Fredericksburg, Groveton, Second Bull Run, Yorktown, and Fairfax in the course of the war, and then resumed his mission to Rome, where he served from 1865 to 1867.*

Q. General Nathaniel Lyon was encamped at Springfield, Missouri, awaiting supplies in early August. The Confederate forces, sensing his weakness, began to gather around him, quickly assembling an army twice the size of Lyon's. What did he do on August 10 at Wilson's Creek?

    a. Retreat northward
    b. Surrender
    c. Attack despite the size of the opposing forces

A. *General Lyon attacked, either out of overconfidence or desperation. He was killed, the battle was a complete victory for the South, and Union movements in Missouri were stymied until the following year.*

Q. At the end of August, General John Frémont, famous as "The Pathfinder of the West," whom Lincoln had named Commander of the Department of the West with headquarters at St. Louis, Missouri, took it upon himself to declare martial law in Missouri, and announced that the property of rebels would be confiscated and their slaves freed. Lincoln was furious, since these actions were not only unauthorized but ran directly counter to Lincoln's attempts to keep the border states in the Union. Who paid an emotional visit to Lincoln on September 10 to plead the general's case?

A. *The general's wife. Her pleas were not heeded, in part because the general continued to defy orders, and Lincoln sent an emissary to remove him from command only six weeks later.*

Q. Within days of one another at the end of September and the beginning of October, Lincoln and Jefferson Davis each held meetings to discuss problems of public pressure. Lincoln met with his Cabinet and General McClellan; Davis met with Generals Johnston, Beauregard, and Smith. The two leaders had exactly the same problem with their respective constituents. What was it that the populace was demanding both North and South?

A. *That a major new offensive be mounted. The Union public wanted a fresh attack on Richmond; the Southern public wanted a major attack on Washington. Both Lincoln and Davis felt the time was not propitious and resisted popular sentiment.*

Q. What peculiarity was shared by such Northern newspapers as the *Brooklyn Eagle, The New York Journal of Daily Commerce,* the New York *Daily News,* and the Essex County *Democrat* in New Jersey?

A. *They were pro-Southern. In mid-August a number of the papers were brought into court on various charges. An editor of the Essex County* Democrat *was also tarred and feathered.*

Q. On September 3, the Confederate general Leonidas Polk captured Columbus, Kentucky, on the Mississippi River. Why was General Polk often referred to as "the Bishop" by his soldiers?

A. *A graduate of West Point, he had resigned from the army to join the Episcopalian clergy. At the outbreak of the war, at*

the special request of Jefferson Davis, he had taken a com-
mand in the Confederate army, at the same time retaining
his office as the Episcopal bishop of New Orleans.

Q. Countering Polk's capture of Columbus, General Ulysses S. Grant took Paducah, Kentucky. What did this strategic move bring an end to?

A. *The possibility that Kentucky could remain a neutral state.*

Q. What did the following events in the first two weeks of October make clear?

1. Two Confederate ships were seized as they tried to slip past the blockade of New Orleans.
2. Confederate attempts to overwhelm Fort Clark and Fort Hatteras on Hatteras Inlet in North Carolina, which were recently taken by the Union, failed.
3. A heavy Confederate attack on Santa Rosa Island off the Florida coast was repulsed by troops from Fort Pickens.
4. The U.S.S. *Richmond* and U.S.S. *Vincennes* were subjected to heavy attack at the mouth of the Mississippi. Even though they were briefly run aground, both were ultimately able to escape.

A. *The Union blockade of the Southern ports was taking a real*
toll on the Confederacy, and even concerted countermea-
sures were unable to disrupt it.

Q. At mid-month, Jefferson Davis was besieged by requests from unhappy Confederate soldiers. What did they want?

a. Leave to see their families
b. Improved supplies
c. To rejoin their individual state militias

A. *The answer is* c, *pointing up the degree to which the Southern population was devoted to the defense of their native states as much as to an overall Confederate "cause."*

Q. What was held for the first time in the Confederacy on November 6, 1861?

A. *A general election. Under the new constitution, Jefferson Davis was elected to a six-year term along with Alexander Stephens as vice-president.*

Q. To persuade the British and French to back the Confederacy, two envoys were dispatched abroad, James M. Mason of Virginia to Great Britain and John Slidell of Louisiana to France. They managed to run the blockade to Havana, where they embarked on the British mail steamer, the *Trent.* On November 8, Captain Charles S. Wilkes of the *San Jacinto,* a Union war sloop, stopped the *Trent* and removed the Confederate envoys, whom he then took to Boston and had imprisoned. Which of the following took the strongest stand against this action?

    a. The Confederacy
    b. France
    c. Great Britain

A. *Great Britain. It was, after all, their ship that had been stopped. The British public was in an uproar, the British government dispatched troops to Canada, and the foreign secretary issued an ultimatum demanding the release of Mason and Slidell with safe passage to England.*

Q. Lincoln and Secretary of State William H. Seward realized that they had a grave diplomatic crisis on their hands because of the *Trent* affair. Since the actions of Captain Wilkes had not been authorized, why didn't Lincoln simply comply with the British ultimatum?

A. *Because Captain Wilkes had been hailed in the North as a great hero; both public opinion and Congress were adamantly against releasing the envoys.*

Q. After considerable delay Lincoln and Seward were forced to release Mason and Slidell. But they placated Northern opinion by pointing out that the British had now agreed in principle that civilians could not be considered a contraband of war. Why was this a master stroke?

A. *Because that was precisely the issue over which the United States had gone to war with Great Britain in the War of 1812.*

Q. In early November, General Winfield Scott relinquished command of the Union army and General McClellan was chosen to replace him. McClellan was given a huge torchlight parade in Washington on November 11. On the night of the thirteenth, Lincoln paid a call at McClellan's Washington home to discuss strategy with him. What occurred that gave credence to suggestions that the young general's extremely rapid rise to the highest command had swelled his head?

A. *He retired for the night without seeing the president.*

Q. On May 20, North Carolina had officially seceded from the Union. On November 18, delegates from forty-two North Carolina counties met at Hatteras in a special convention to do what in regard to the May 20 secession order?

A. *This large group of pro-Union North Carolinians voted to repudiate the secession vote, and two days later appointed Marble Nash Taylor as provisional governor. Thus North Carolina, like Missouri, had two rival governments.*

Q. At Wheeling in western Virginia, what was formally adopted on November 26?

A. *A constitution for the new state.*

Q. On December 1, the U.S. gunboat *Penguin* captured a Confederate blockade runner called the *Albion*. What was the value of the military equipment found aboard?

    a. $25,000
    b. $50,000
    c. $100,000

A. *The answer is c.*

Q. The Congress of the Confederacy voted to admit Kentucky as a state on December 10. Had Kentucky in fact seceded?

A. *No. The new Confederate flag adopted after First Manassas had thirteen stars, including stars for Kentucky and Missouri, but neither state ever officially seceded from the Union.*

Q. On the twentieth, sixteen old whaling ships were sunk in the waters outside the harbor of Charleston, South Carolina, in order to further impede blockade runners. What had happened to Charleston four days earlier that made this action particularly easy to carry out?

A. *In a blaze that had no connection with the war, half of Charleston had been burned to the ground. This event brought the first year of the Civil War to a close on a dismal note for the Southern cause.*

Part Three
1862

Q. The second year of the war opened with President Lincoln once again trying to get his generals to do something, writing letters to both General Don Carlos Buell in Kentucky and General Halleck in Missouri. McClellan was sidelined in Washington, recovering from what appears to have been typhoid fever. On the Confederate side, however, what general moved out and destroyed miles of railway lines and telegraph wires along the Potomac?

A. *Stonewall Jackson started off with a bang in a year that would see him cause endless problems for the Union. After his forays against the rail lines, he took Romney in western Virginia, and set up a winter camp.*

Q. Secretary of War Simon Cameron, who had been promised a Cabinet job by Lincoln's managers at the 1860 Republican Convention, offered his resignation in early January. Lincoln, who had been dismayed by the deal, was glad to see Cameron go, since his administration had been riddled with corruption and marked by military failure. Lincoln chose Edwin Stanton, a Washington lawyer who had been attorney general at the end of the Buchanan administration. Was Stanton a strong supporter of Lincoln?

A. *No. He had been critical, sometimes harshly so. He was a Democrat, but anti-slavery, and Lincoln wanted a Democrat in the Cabinet to give his administration a more "national" look. Stanton was also a personal friend of McClellan, and Lincoln thought he might be able to handle the slow-to-move general.*

Q. A Union army of 4,000 men, led by General George H. Thomas, that had been advancing into Kentucky over the mountains was attacked by a Confederate force of the same size on January 19 in the battle of Mill Springs, also known as Logan's Cross Roads. Because troops under General Felix Zollicoffer were badly positioned, the Confederates were routed by the forces of General Thomas. Zollicoffer was killed, and Thomas captured more than 1,000 horses, 100 wagons, and other supplies. Was General Thomas greatly cheered in the North for this victory, which solidified the Union presence in the area for a year?

A. *Only in some quarters. A great many Northerners were suspicious of General Thomas and openly questioned his loyalty, simply because he was a Virginian and had been a friend of General Lee. Despite his splendid record, it was not until 1864 that Thomas was fully accepted in the North as a Union patriot.*

Q. What did Federal naval forces do in the harbor of Charleston, South Carolina, during the third week of January in an attempt to foil blockade-running confederate vessels?

A. *They sank a number of ships laden with stones in order to make navigation perilous.*

Q. On January 27, Lincoln issued General War Order Number One. It called for what to happen on February 22?

A. *It ordered that the twenty-second "be the day for a general movement of the Land and Naval forces of the United States against the insurgent forces." Lincoln was fed up with delays by General McClellan in mounting a concerted attack against the South. McClellan was a genius at organization, but wanted to have an extremely fine-tuned military machine before he made a strong offensive move. McClellan would in fact ignore the order.*

Q. Swedish-born ship designer John Ericsson oversaw the launching of what vessel at the Greenpoint, Long Island, shipyards on January 30?

A. *The ironclad* Monitor.

Q. On the sixth of February, Confederate General Lloyd Tilghman sent all but about 60 of his 3,000 troops from the base at Fort Henry in Tennessee to the larger Fort Donelson twelve miles to the east as Union land and river forces closed in. Which of the following was his greatest worry?

    a.   The expectation that the opposing forces would be much larger than his
    b.   Concern that the powder for the Confederate guns was inferior and dangerous
    c.   Increasing worry about rising flood waters

A. *The answer is c, although both other factors played a part in his decision. But the flooding was his chief concern, correctly; within two days the waters would have covered the fort's powder magazine. Tilghman remained behind in order to stall the Union advance for at least an hour, but it was two hours before Fort Henry was taken.*

Q. While Union troops were massing around Fort Donelson in Tennessee, a Union force of 7,500 under General Ambrose was able to take an important North Carolina Atlantic coast island that had been an early English settlement. What was the island's name?

A. *Roanoke Island, which was occupied by Union forces on February 8, costing the Confederacy a very important stronghold.*

Q. Fort Donelson had been erected on a bluff above the Cumberland River, some seventy feet above the waterline, near Dover, Tennessee. Why was this fort a very significant military target for the North?

A. *The Cumberland River and the Tennessee River, where Fort Henry was located, were both of great importance to the movement of both commerce and military equipment in the South. Over their combined length they were nearly as vital as the Mississippi. For that reason, the alternative name for the Battle of Fort Donelson is the Battle of Two Rivers.*

Q. The forces of General Grant that surrounded Fort Donelson numbered 40,000. How many Confederate soldiers manned the fort?

a. 12,000
b. 18,000
c. 24,000

A. *The answer is b. General Gideon Pillow and General John Floyd decided to try to break through Union lines and open an escape route to Nashville. This was successful, but General Pillow thought the Union forces were in full retreat themselves, and made a fatal attempt to chase after them. Both General Pillow and General Floyd ultimately left the battle area in small boats, fearful that they would be shot as traitors rather than considered prisoners of war. Both were subsequently removed from their commands by Jefferson Davis.*

Q. There were still troops at Fort Donelson, however. Pillow and Floyd had left General Simon Bolivar Buckner, whom they outranked, to surrender the fort itself. He sent a message to Grant asking to discuss terms. Grant replied with a famous phrase that President Roosevelt and Winston Churchill would also use in World War II in respect to Germany and Japan. What Did Grant demand in his reply on February 16?

A. *"Unconditional surrender." The phrase struck a deep chord in the North and greatly increased Grant's popularity. From then on he was often called Unconditional Surrender Grant rather than Ulysses Simpson Grant. General Buckner complied, and Grant, realizing that Buckner had behaved with much greater honor than his superiors, offered to lend him money, even though he would be a prisoner of war, an offer that was graciously refused. He was exchanged for a Union general several months later.*

Q. Was Ulysses Simpson Grant the name the general was given at birth?

A. *No. He was christened Hiram Ulysses Grant, but a mistake was made by the politician who recommended him to West Point.*

Q. The only bright spot for the South in the disaster at Fort Donelson was the escape of a thirty-nine-year-old colonel and his cavalry troops, a battalion this self-made millionaire had raised at his own expense. He went on to become one of the most famous figures of the Civil War. Name him.

A. *Nathan Bedford Forrest.*

Q. President and Mrs. Lincoln suffered a personal tragedy on the twentieth of February. What was it?

A. *The third of their four sons, William Wallace Lincoln, whom they called Willie, died of typhoid fever at the age of twelve. They had lost another son, Edward Baker Lincoln, before the war, but the imaginative Willie was their favorite, and his death hit Mary Lincoln particularly hard. She never again set foot in the room where he died, although she did hold a séance at the White House in an attempt to contact him.*

Q. In February of 1862, the wife of Dr. Samuel Gridley Howe published a song in *The Atlantic,* which paid her four dollars for the verses set to the tune of "John Brown's Body." What was this famous song called?

A. *Julia Ward Howe's "The Battle Hymn of the Republic" became a favorite with Union troops within two months.*

Q. What was immediately dubbed a "cheesebox on a raft" by the press?

A. *The U.S.S.* Monitor, *Ericsson's ironclad, which was launched on January 30, and commissioned on March 4.*

Q. On March 8, Washington was thrown into turmoil by news of action in Chesapeake Bay. A captured Union vessel was causing havoc, ramming and sinking the sailing sloop *Cumberland,* and driving aground and setting on fire the fifty-gun frigate *Congress.* Secretary of War Stanton was in virtual panic. What was the ship that was causing all the commotion, and what had the Confederates renamed her?

A. *The ironclad* Merrimack, *which the Confederates had raised, refitted, and named the* Virginia.

Q. Even as Stanton was running to the window to see whether the *Virginia* was steaming up the river to attack Washington itself, where was the *Monitor?*

A. *By pure coincidence it was within earshot of the battle in Chesapeake Bay. It got to the area by nightfall, rescued some of the crew members of the* Congress, *and waited for dawn. The* Virginia *was spotted a little after 7:00 A.M., and an hour later the two ships engaged in the historic first battle between ironclads. After four hours, the two ships withdrew, the battle a draw.*

Q. General Earl Van Dorn of Mississippi developed a plan to lead a force of 16,000 troops through Missouri to capture St. Louis and then attack General Grant's forces from the north. But first he had to get past a small Union force of 11,000 at Pea Ridge on the Arkansas-Missouri border. He decided to move his army, which included three regiments of Indians, around the Union force and attack it from the rear. Name the legendary gunslinger of the Old West who was among the Union scouts who picked up on the movement and warned the Union commander, Samuel R. Curtis.

A. *James Butler "Wild Bill" Hickok; much of his claimed participation in the Civil War is suspect, but this was one site where he was present. During the night of March 6–7, Cur-*

The Civil War Quiz Book

tis turned his army around. The Confederate generals Ben McCulloch and James McIntosh (whose brother John was a Union general) were both killed the following day as the battle moved to the area of Elkhorn Tavern, and the larger Confederate army was routed and scattered.

Q. The Hungarian-born Union general, Alexander (Sándor) As-both, was wounded at Pea Ridge. What faithful companion had accompanied him into battle?

A. *His dog, York. A drawing of the general and his staff on horseback with York running alongside just prior to the battle of Pea Ridge appeared in* Leslie's Weekly.

Q. On March 11, President Lincoln removed General McClellan from his position as General-in-Chief of the Union army, and assigned him to the Army of the Potomac. Whom did he appoint to succeed McClellan as General-in-Chief?

A. *No one at this juncture. All generals, including McClellan, were under the orders of Secretary of War Edwin Stanton.*

Q. A Missouri town that was the focus of a major, but anticlimactic, earthquake scare in 1990 was captured by General John Pope after being evacuated by Confederates on March 13. Name the town.

A. *New Madrid. This put the Union army in a good position to attack the Confederate stronghold in the Mississippi River, Island Number Ten. But it would not be easy. Withdrawing from a threatened position at Columbus, Ohio, Confederate general Leonidas Polk moved 140 pieces of heavy artillery down to Island Number Ten, and greatly strengthened its garrison.*

1862

Q. Name the future president who was appointed military governor of Tennessee by Lincoln in March of 1862.

A. *Andrew Johnson.*

Q. General Grant's troops were encamped at Pittsburg Landing on the Tennessee River near the town of Shiloh in mid-March. Why was General Grant not with them until the seventeenth of March?

A. *General Halleck had relieved Grant of command, on the grounds that Grant had not answered official telegrams, while at the same time suggesting that Grant's old drinking problems had returned. Grant said that he had never received the telegrams, leading to stories that the telegraph operator was a spy for the Confederacy. This is an extremely clouded situation, but many historians have suggested that Halleck was simply jealous of Grant. He finally backed off, and after ten days in limbo, Grant's command was restored to him on the fifteenth.*

Q. How far was Pittsburg Landing from General Johnston's Confederate stronghold across the border at Corinth, Mississippi?

A. *Only twenty miles.*

Q. What had General Johnston learned that caused him to decide that it was urgent to attack Grant's forces in early April?

A. *He had received information that the 20,000 troops under General Don Carlos Buell at Nashville, Tennessee, had been ordered to join Grant's 37,000 at Pittsburg Landing. There were also another 5,000 Union troops a few miles north of*

Pittsburg Landing at Crump. Johnston had 40,000 troops with another 15,000 coming to join them. If he could attack Grant before Buell arrived, he would have a 7,000-man advantage, but once Buell got in place that would turn into a 2,000-man disadvantage.

Q. The Confederate attack on Grant was set for the morning of April 5. Why did it have to be postponed until the following day?

A. *Heavy rains turned the dirt roads into sloughs of mud, causing a fateful loss of time.*

Q. How prepared were Grant's forces for the attack at dawn on April 6?

A. *Utterly unprepared. They were just waking or cooking breakfast and an extraordinary lapse in reconnaissance by the Union forces allowed Johnston's troops to spend the night only two miles away without detection. One colonel, Everett Peabody, had the wits to send out a small scouting party at 3:00 A.M., and when shots were exchanged with Confederate troops, a late warning was given.*

Q. As the full-scale Confederate attack began, how close had General Buell's 20,000 men gotten to Pittsburg Landing?

A. *They were seven miles away across the Tennessee River. The twenty-four hour delay in the attack had brought them close enough to come to the aid of Grant.*

Q. What did the phrase "seeing the elephant" mean to the soldiers on both sides at Shiloh?

A. *It was a popular phrase to describe the shock of experiencing actual combat for the first time. Many of the troops on both sides at Shiloh had never been in battle before, and both armies were weakened by the number of troops that broke and ran.*

Q. Although General William Tecumseh Sherman was forced to order his troops to retreat again and again at Shiloh, he made a great impression on General Grant. How so?

A. *He held each position stubbornly, retreating only when the position became untenable, and thus helped to buy time for the Union forces. In addition, he showed great courage, riding back and forth ceaselessly among his men, undeterred by two slight wounds or the fact that three horses were shot out from under him in the course of the long day. His future was forged that April 6, both because he came to terms with himself as a man, and because Grant recognized what Sherman had to offer and would thus count on him more and more as time went on.*

Q. At 2:30 in the afternoon, even as his forces were making great headway against the Union army, General Johnston was badly wounded. From what consequence of the wound did he die?

A. *He bled to death. General Beauregard took over as commander.*

Q. What were the Owl, the Snake, and the Lick, and why did they present the Union army with a serious problem at Shiloh?

A. *They were three creeks that put the Union forces in a box. The Confederate plan was to attack through the only land exit from the box, but the Confederates did not assign spe-cific responsibility for clearly delineated segments of the line of attack, in part because the thick woods made both com-munication and the maneuvering of troops difficult.*

Q. Union forces were soon in retreat all along the line, and General Grant could only hope that the forces of General Buell, as well as those camped seven miles away at Crump, could get to the area around Shiloh Meeting House in time to prevent a disaster. But before reinforcements could ar-rive, the Union forces were able to form a strong new line. What made this possible?

A. *At the center of the Union position there was a configuration of dense woods with open fields to either side, with a sunken road running along the front, that provided a natural de-fensive position. From the confines of the woods, the re-maining forces were able to repulse one Confederate attack after another with such a fusillade of shots that the area came to be called the "hornet's nest."*

Q. Which of the following did *not* happen in the hour before sunset at Shiloh on the first day of the battle?

    a. General Prentiss surrendered the remaining 2,200 troops of the 4,500 who had been holding their ground at the "hornet's nest."

    b. The first troops of General Buell's forces as well as those that had been stationed upriver at Crump arrived at the battle site.

    c. General Beauregard ordered his Confederate forces to make one final assault in the twilight.

A. *The answer is c. Although he did not know at the time that Union reinforcements were arriving, Beauregard felt that his men did not have another assault left in them and decided not to follow up on Prentiss's surrender.*

Q. Despite the fact that the Union forces had had 7,000 men killed or wounded on April 6, they were the stronger army by the following morning. How many reinforcements had arrived?

    a. 15,000
    b. 25,000
    c. 30,000

A. *The answer is b. Although they were very late in getting to Shiloh, the fresh Union forces would be enough to repel the Confederate army. Expected Confederate forces never arrived at all.*

Q. Violent rainstorms broke during the night and continued for hours, making it almost impossible for the exhausted men on both sides to get any sleep. The 10,000 wounded men from the two armies spent the night in agony. Where did General Grant pass the night?

A. *Refusing to take shelter on a steamboat, Grant spent the night in the field among his men. General Beauregard, however, slept in the captured tent that had belonged to General Sherman.*

Q. At first light on April 7, a second surprise attack was launched. Who made it?

A. *This time it was the Union forces, both the fresh forces of General Buell and those of Grant's Army of Western Tennessee. They made very quick headway at first, driving the*

Confederate forces back in disarray. Then the Confederate forces made a strong stand again, but by midafternoon, with no sign of reinforcements, General Beauregard ordered a retreat back to Corinth.

Q. Did the Union army continue forward once the Confederates began retreating?

A. *No, they were far too exhausted to do so.*

Q. Brigadier General Alexander McDowell McCook was among those who reinforced Grant at Shiloh. How many members of the McCook family served in the Union army during the Civil War?

    a. 7
    b. 11
    c. 16

A. *The answer is c. Still another served in the navy. General Alexander McCook's father and nine brothers, as well as his uncle and his uncle's five sons all fought for the Union cause. Two of Alexander's brothers, Daniel junior and Robert L., also became generals, as did a cousin, Edward Moody McCook. Robert died from a bullet fired by one of General Forrest's irregulars, Frank Gurley, on August 2, 1862, while urging on the horses drawing the ambulance he had been riding in. In the North, Gurley was regarded as a murderer and twice came close to being hanged. Daniel junior was seriously wounded at Kennesaw Mountain, leading an attack he knew to be virtually suicidal, and died on July 16, one day after being promoted to brigadier general. Few families contributed more to the Union cause than the McCooks of Ohio.*

Q. There were two Union generals named Wallace at Shiloh. The first, William Harvey Lamb Wallace, was a hero of the first day of the battle, holding a position at the "hornet's nest" for six hours, which made it possible for the Union forces to regroup after the surprise attack. As he was withdrawing his men, he was shot through the eye and died on April 10. The other General Wallace fell victim to confusing orders and did not arrive from Crump until the battle was almost over. He was made a scapegoat for the tremendous loss of life and relieved of his command. Later in the war he successfully defended Cincinnati, and was one of those named to serve as a judge at the court-martial of the Lincoln assassination conspirators. But his greatest fame was to come with the publication in 1880 of a novel on a biblical theme that was to become one of the most widely read books of the century. Name the general and his novel.

A. *General Lewis "Lew" Wallace went on to write* Ben Hur: A Tale of the Christ.

Q. This Confederate private was captured at Shiloh and subsequently joined the Union army as a self-described "galvanized Yankee." In later life he would achieve worldwide fame and utter what are probably the most quoted words ever spoken on the African continent. Name him.

A. *Henry Morton Stanley, who would one day say, "Dr. Livingstone, I presume."*

Q. What does the biblical name *Shiloh* actually mean?

A. *It means "place of peace," an ironic name for the site of the war's bloodiest battle yet, with a total of more than 20,000 killed or wounded, with slightly heavier casualties on the Union side. In both the North and the South, the public was for the first time shocked into an awareness that the war would be long and terrible.*

Q. Name the other future U.S. president, aside from Grant, who was at Shiloh.

A. *Brigadier General James Abram Garfield, who was the commander of the 20th Brigade of the 6th Division of the Army of the Ohio, was one of the last of the reinforcements under General Buell to arrive on the scene, and his brigade saw only minimal combat on the seventh of April.*

Q. The Confederate forces at Island Number Ten in the Mississippi surrendered to General John Pope's troops on the same day as the Confederate retreat from Shiloh. This almost bloodless victory had been made possible by a construction project. What was it?

A. *The heavily armed garrison at Island Number Ten had cut off Union shipping on the Mississippi, but General Pope had a canal dug around it. This was possible because the garrison was located near a bulge of land around which the river curved on both sides. This allowed the movement of both troops and supplies. On the fourth of April, a gunboat provided by Commodore Andrew H. Foote, the* Carondelet, *ran the garrison on the Mississippi itself during a heavy thunderstorm, followed by the gunboat* Pittsburgh *two nights later. The island was now surrounded, and nearly 7,000 Confederate troops, including three generals, were forced to surrender. Thousands of guns and hundreds of horses were also taken. General Pope achieved heroic stature in the North overnight.*

Q. General Halleck then had Pope join Grant and Buell at Pittsburg Landing. What would Halleck, Grant, Sherman, and a young captain named Philip Sheridan, also at Pittsburg Landing, eventually have in common?

A. *They would all become General-in-Chief of the United States Army.*

Q. How did General Halleck ''reward'' Grant for his success in repulsing the Confederate attack at Shiloh?

A. *He made him second in command, under himself, of the combined forces at Pittsburg Landing. But this really meant that Buell and Pope, in command of their own forces, had more standing. Halleck still underrated Grant, as well as disliking him.*

Q. The rifled musket was the mainstay of troops on both sides during the Civil War. These powder-and-ball guns had to be reloaded after each shot. How many shots per minute was regarded as a fast rate?

    a. Two
    b. Three
    c. Four

A. *The answer is b. But that pace could not be kept up steadily, since the bore of the gun needed to be cleaned after only a few shots to maintain firing accuracy.*

Q. Newspaper headlines were made in both the North and the South by a daring raid in mid-April that led to the hijacking of *The General*. What was *The General?*

A. *A train locomotive. One James J. Andrews, a spy of cloudy background, led twenty-two Ohio soldiers on an unauthorized foray into Georgia. Dressed as civilians, they boarded a train at Marietta, Georgia. When the westbound train stopped for breakfast the following morning, April 12, they disconnected the passenger cars and took off aboard* The General *with three boxcars still attached, heading into Tennessee. The idea was to inflict damage on the line, but they were immediately pursued in another locomotive and, running low on fuel, abandoned the effort after traveling about ninety miles. All were eventually captured and a third of the men were hanged, including Andrews.*

Q. Because of manpower problems, the Confederate Congress passed an act on April 16 that was the first of its kind in American history. What was it?

A. *It established a general conscription (draft) law. The Union did not follow suit until nearly a year later.*

Q. "Whatever is to be done should be done quickly. The forts must be run." Who wrote these words concerning Fort Jackson and Fort St. Philip on the banks of the Mississippi below New Orleans?

A. *Flag Officer David Glasgow Farragut, as he prepared his fleet to try to slip past the forts at night in order to take New Orleans from the Confederates. Obstructions had been placed in the river and there were no land forces to attack the forts from the rear, but his daring plan worked. After managing to clear part of a chain-link barrier, his fleet sailed under the forts. The surprised Confederate troops opened up with heavy fire, but Farragut had gotten just far enough to be able to continue through the night of April 24. New Orleans was seized the next day and formally surrendered on the twenty-ninth.*

Q. Farragut was named a rear admiral in July as a reward for his capture of New Orleans. After the war, in 1866, he was the first man in United States history to attain what status?

A. *He was the first full admiral in American history. Before him, no one had risen higher than vice admiral.*

Q. By the twenty-seventh, six Confederate-held forts in the New Orleans vicinity surrendered, including Forts Jackson and St. Philip. What was unique, however, about the fall of Fort Jackson?

A. *The troops mutinied and many fled before the surrender.*

Q. General Joseph Johnston's Confederate troops evacuated Yorktown, Virginia, on May 3. The town had been under siege for a full month by General McClellan's Army of the Potomac. By how great a margin did Union forces outnumber Confederate troops?

    a. 2 to 1
    b. 4 to 1
    c. 5 to 1

A. *The answer is b. Even though reinforcements had been brought in, the 100,000 Union troops massed in the area constituted far too vast an army for Johnston to risk a full-fledged battle. As it was, more than 1,700 Confederate troops were lost in the process of abandoning Yorktown.*

Q. On May 8, General Stonewall Jackson and 9,000 men fought a Union force of about 5,000 at the village of McDowell, near Staunton, Virginia, in the Shenandoah Valley, and won decisively. Jackson had misled the Union scouts by seeming to head toward Richmond, but had doubled back on railway cars from a point near Charlottesville. Why was General Robert E. Lee particularly pleased with this victory?

A. *It had been Lee's belief that it was essential to keep the Union forces constantly off guard, so as to prevent them from massing on more important fronts, particularly around Richmond at that time. The forces Jackson defeated were actually part of an army General Frémont was putting together to march on Knoxville, Tennessee. Jackson's victory not only totally disrupted that plan but also gave additional pause to Lincoln about supplying General McClellan on the Richmond front with additional troops. This was the first proof that Lee's strategy of distraction, which he would use throughout the rest of the war, would work.*

Q. The Confederates evacuated a major Southern naval port on the ninth of May. Name it.

A. *Norfolk, Virginia. Despite efforts to destroy as many supplies as possible, the Union troops were left with a considerable bounty when they occupied Norfolk on the tenth.*

Q. Many Confederate vessels from Norfolk beat a retreat along the James River toward Richmond. But the most important single vessel that had been anchored at Norfolk had to be blown up and scuttled in order to prevent it from being captured by Union forces. What was the name of the vessel and why was it unable to sail up the James River?

A. *The ironclad* Virginia, *formerly the* Merrimack, *was regarded as far too unwieldy to navigate the James River, although smaller ironclads would be used extensively by both sides along inland waterways throughout the war. Without ocean swells to contend with, ironclad gunboats did very well.*

Q. Why did near-panic break out in the Confederate capital of Richmond on May 15?

A. *News of Union gunboats moving up the James River toward the city became general knowledge.*

Q. Jefferson Davis had declared that Richmond must be defended at all costs. He felt that if Richmond fell, the credibility of the Confederacy would collapse with it, ensuring that none of the European countries whose aid was still hoped for would any longer take the Southern effort seriously. In addition, he knew that if Richmond fell, the South would suffer a perhaps mortal blow to the morale of Confederate citizens and soldiers. But there was also a third, purely practical, reason for defending Richmond to the death. What was it?

A. *Richmond was the hub of iron manufacturing in the South, with the Tedegar Iron Works the major source of cannon for the war. Other companies produced pistols, rifles, and cartridges; one Richmond company alone manufactured more than 70 million cartridges in the course of the war.*

Q. The commanding general of occupied New Orleans issued an order on the sixteenth that brought him a new nickname in the South: ''Beast Butler.'' What was the order?

A. *The occupying troops of New Orleans had been much harassed by its women, who assumed that as members of the fairer sex they could get away with such behavior, but Butler retaliated with what came to be known as the ''Woman Order.'' In it, he suggested that they were not the ''ladies'' they called themselves, and went on to state: ''Hereafter when any female shall by word, gesture or movement insult or show contempt for any officer or soldier of the United States, she shall be regarded and held liable to be treated as a woman of the town plying her avocation.'' Union troops were severely warned not to try to use the order as an excuse for misconduct, but that hardly mattered. Southern honor had been insulted and Butler became loathed beyond measure.*

Q. On May 9, General David Hunter, who was close to Lincoln personally, had used his command of the Department of the South to issue an order pertaining to the states of South Carolina, Georgia, and Florida that Lincoln felt compelled to countermand ten days later, on May 19. What was Hunter's order?

A. *Without consulting Lincoln and without any mandate from Congress, Hunter had declared the slaves in the three states to be free. Hunter had a checkered career during the rest of the war, but was among those who accompanied the body of Lincoln back to Illinois for burial following the president's assassination.*

Q. General McClellan's Army of the Potomac had closed to within ten miles of Richmond by the end of the third week in May. Even so, he continued to pressure Lincoln for additional troops from the forces of General Irvin McDowell, who was charged with defending Washington. How many troops did General McClellan in fact already have near Richmond?

   a. 80,000
   b. 85,000
   c. 102,000

A. *According to McClellan's own reports, the numbers were any of the above. He changed them from day to day, with the number actually decreasing even after new troops had arrived. Lincoln compared dispatching troops to McClellan to "shoveling fleas across a barnyard," but nevertheless he*

*agreed on the eighteenth to send another 35,000 men under
General McDowell.*

Q. What caused Lincoln to rescind the order for McDowell to
join McClellan on May 24?

A. *In another of his surprise maneuvers, Stonewall Jackson
had taken Front Royal, Virginia, the previous day. Lincoln
instead ordered McDowell and General Frémont to go after
Jackson, who once again had implemented Lee's strategy to
perfection.*

Q. One of the keys to Stonewall Jackson's successes in the
Shenandoah Valley was a transplanted New Yorker named
Jedediah Hotchkiss. What was he?

   a. A Confederate spy
   b. A munitions expert
   c. A mapmaker

A. *Hotchkiss was a mapmaker, one of the great topographers
of his time. With a special genius for finding unlikely routes
to a given place, he was a perfect match for Jackson's
strategic brilliance at turning up where he was least expected. Later in the war General Lee also relied upon him
heavily. He was arrested after the war, but General Grant
personally arranged his release and the return of his maps,
which were subsequently used in the official records of the
Civil War.*

Q. On the twenty-fifth, Jackson attacked General Nathaniel
Banks at his base at Winchester, Virginia, to which he had
quickly retreated after Jackson took Front Royal. The Union

troops were outnumbered by more than two to one, and the 6,000 Union soldiers were quickly routed. Why was Banks derisively called "Commissary Banks" by the Confederates following this battle?

A. *Because in the helter-skelter retreat from Winchester, huge supplies of food and medical stores were left behind. In addition, Jackson got his hands on 9,000 rifles and took 2,000 prisoners.*

Q. Why did Stonewall Jackson make Belle Boyd an honorary captain in the Confederate Army?

A. *Using her father's hotel as a base, Belle Boyd provided invaluable services as a spy during the Shenandoah Valley campaign in the spring of 1862. She was arrested and released twice during the war, went to England to recover from typhoid, and then fell in love with and married the Union naval officer who captured the blockade runner on which she was trying to return to the South. Her husband, Samuel Hardinge, was cashiered from the navy for allowing Belle to escape back to England, and died before the war was over. In England Belle published a book about her experiences and developed a stage career there.*

Q. Why did Jackson pull back from the Harpers Ferry area following his defeat of Banks?

A. *He had learned that General Frémont was marching from the west and General James Shields from the east on the same route with the intention of cutting his forces off. He was gone by the time Frémont and Shields met up, and Shields was left with the minor compensation of retaking Front Royal. Jackson had once again succeeded in forcing the Union forces to change their plans entirely.*

Q. General Halleck, who was widely referred to as "Old
Brains"—not because of his age, which was only forty-
seven, but because of his knowledge of military history and
adherence to the "book"—started to march nearly 120,000
men toward Corinth, Mississippi, which was held by General Beauregard and 70,000 Confederate troops. Corinth was
a crucial point on the railroad to Memphis. It was finally
taken by Halleck on May 30, a month after he had started
out from Pittsburg Landing. How far was Corinth from Pittsburg Landing and why did it take so long for Halleck's
forces to reach it?

A. *The distance was only about forty-five miles, but Halleck
insisted that his troops dig in every evening, in case Beauregard should decide to attack. As a result, his forces almost
never moved forward more than two miles a day and usually
not more than one. When Beauregard finally decided to
abandon Corinth on May 25, he had plenty of time to withdraw.*

Q. Aside from the fact that he was seriously outnumbered,
Beauregard had another reason to get out of Corinth that had
to do with the state of the city itself. What was it?

A. *It had an inadequate water supply, much of which had become contaminated, and there was a continually escalating
loss of life from disease, rising into the low thousands.*

Q. On May 31, at the urging of Jefferson Davis, General Joseph Eggleston Johnston (no relation to General Albert S.
Johnston, who had been mortally wounded at Shiloh)
made an attack on part of the Union army just outside
Richmond itself. The battle, called Fair Oaks by Northerners and Seven Pines by Southerners, initially seemed to
offer advantages to the Confederates because of something

that had happened to the Chickahominy River just north of Richmond. What was it?

A. *Because of a very wet spring and a drenching storm on the thirtieth, the Chickahominy had flooded, washing out many of the temporary bridges that McClellan had had built to connect the two wings of his army, which were camped on both sides of the river. The splitting of McClellan's army is widely regarded by historians as a serious tactical mistake on McClellan's part, but on this particular day the Confederates were unable to take advantage of it. Although they were attacking the weaker left wing south of the river, the attack was badly coordinated, and the wooded marshy terrain was so inhospitable that the Confederate losses of 6,000 were hardly worth the effort. The Union forces suffered a thousand fewer casualties, and although they pulled back some the next day, the threat to Richmond remained.*

Q. General Johnston was severely wounded at Seven Pines. Whom did Davis select to replace him?

A. *General Robert E. Lee was named the commander of the Army of Northern Virginia.*

Q. Were Southerners pleased with the appointment of Lee?

A. *No. In many quarters he was called ''Evacuating Lee'' because in several instances he had withdrawn rather than pit his men against overwhelming forces. At this point in the war Lee was both misunderstood and underrated on both sides. McClellan was delighted with Lee's appointment, deeming him an excessively ''cautious'' leader—which was, of course, exactly Lincoln's complaint about McClellan.*

Q. Lee was in fact planning a bold stroke. In order to get a better picture of the disposition of McClellan's forces, Lee conceived a daring raid right around the Union army. To lead this expedition he chose a twenty-nine-year-old cavalry officer who had risen quickly to the rank of brigadier general and who was probably the most colorful personality in the Confederate ranks, sporting a red-lined cap with yellow sash and a hat with an ostrich-feather plume. Who was he?

A. *James Ewell Brown "Jeb" Stuart had in mid-October of 1859 carried the orders to Lee to crush John Brown at Harpers Ferry, and had personally read the ultimatum to Brown before the attack. Now, in the second week of June 1862, Lee had an assignment for him that would prove crucial to the defense of Richmond.*

Q. On June 1, a proclamation made by President Lincoln on May 12, concerning the ports of Beaufort in North Carolina, Port Royal in South Carolina, and New Orleans, took effect. What was the intent of the proclamation?

A. *It was to reopen these three ports to commercial traffic now that they were in Union hands, ending the blockade in these areas.*

Q. On June 6, a Confederate naval force was defeated at Memphis, Tennessee, by a Union flotilla that included nine ships that were unarmed. These nine ships, however, were essential to the Union victory. What were they?

A. *They were rams, an instrument of naval warfare that had been used by the ancient Romans, but which had virtually disappeared in the "modern" era of sailing ships. A Pennsylvania engineer with great experience in building locks*

*and dams had the idea that steamships outfitted as rams
would have both the speed and maneuverability to be very
effective against gunboats. Charles Ellet, Jr., couldn't get
the U.S. Navy to pay any attention to his idea, but he managed to get an audience with Secretary of War Edwin Stanton, who saw the possibilities and gave the go-ahead for a
special unit outside the regular navy. Ellet converted nine
steamships and had them manned by eight other members of
his family and specially commissioned riverboat men. Accompanied by regular navy gunboats, they thoroughly defeated the Confederate Navy at Memphis. Only one
Confederate ship escaped, and the city, thousands of whose
citizens watched the battle from the river bluffs, surrendered
to the Union forces. Ironically, Colonel Ellet died two weeks
later of a wound received in the battle, but the unit continued under the command of his brother Alfred and subsequently his son Charles Rivers Ellet, who was made a
colonel at the age of nineteen.*

Q. Following the battles of Front Royal and Winchester on May
23–25, two Union divisions, one under the command of
General Frémont, the other led by General James Shields,
started in pursuit of Stonewall Jackson. How difficult a time
did they have catching up with him?

A. *They were unable to catch him until he decided he was
ready, and turned to confront them. Jackson's men had
become famous for their rapid marching, to the extent that
they were nicknamed the "foot cavalry." On June 8, General Richard Ewell of Jackson's army held off the advance of
General Frémont even though Frémont's 10,500 men outnumbered Ewell's force by 4,000. This battle at Cross Keys,
Virginia, made it impossible for Frémont to join up with
Shields, and the latter was badly defeated by Jackson himself the next day at Port Republic.*

Q. Jeb Stuart led 1,200 cavalrymen toward the northeast on June 12, crossing the headwaters of the Chickahominy. His troops prevailed easily in skirmishes with Union patrols, including one led by General Philip St. George Cooke, the commander of the cavalry reserve of the army of the Potomac. Stuart was particularly elated to foil the pursuing General Cooke. Why?

A. *He was Stuart's father-in-law—whose decision to remain loyal to the Union had greatly angered Stuart.*

Q. Had Stuart's run around McClellan's complete army been a part of the original plan?

A. *No; but once he discovered the location of the small force McClellan had left on the north side of the Chickahominy, he decided it was safer—and more glorious—to keep going than to try to retrace a route through the now aroused Union forces he had already bypassed. Stuart's forces returned safely to Richmond four days after setting out, having lost only one man and bringing with them nearly 170 prisoners and more than 250 captured horses.*

Q. Stuart's famous ride served to make McClellan aware of deficiencies in his position, but it also demoralized Union troops and gave a tremendous boost to flagging Confederate spirits. It also won Lee new public respect because of a personal aspect of his behavior. What was it?

A. *Lee's son and nephew were among those assigned to ride with Stuart on the dangerous mission.*

Q. In mid-June Lincoln created a new Army of Virginia with General John Pope, who had had such a success at Island

Number Ten, as its commander. Frémont, furious at being placed under Pope, resigned and went to New York, where he awaited another call to duty that never came. Pope, however, was disliked by his officers and men because of his arrogance. His haughtiness got him into trouble almost immediately when he was asked by a reporter where his headquarters would be. What did he reply?

A. *He replied that it would be in the saddle, which led to a wry comment that circulated widely in both the North and the South—it was said that Pope's headquarters were where his hindquarters ought to be.*

Q. On June 15, McClellan's forces near Richmond were reinforced by 12,000 men under the command of General George A. McCall. But McClellan wanted still more. What did Lincoln say McClellan's troops would be unable to do if he gave the general all the troops he wanted?

A. *Lie down. "They would have to sleep standing up," the president said.*

Q. What momentous and very controversial directive did Lincoln first outline on the nineteenth of June 1862?

A. *The Emancipation Proclamation, outlawing slavery in all the rebel states. He was in no way ready to issue it yet, however.*

Q. In late June, Union forces captured something that had been constructed out of material donated by aristocratic Southern women. What was it?

A. *An observation balloon made out of hundreds of silk dresses in all the hues of the rainbow. Southern strategists had taken note of the usefulness of the hot-air balloons of Thaddeus Lowe, one of which had given advance warning to Union forces at Seven Pines. But this magical creation they had labored so hard to construct never even got to its first destination. Confederates were outraged, to the extent that even after the war General Longstreet wrote, "This capture was the meanest trick of the war and one that I have never forgiven."*

Q. General Lee had decided that the only hope of preventing McClellan from taking Richmond was to attack the Army of the Potomac, particularly the more isolated smaller force that Jeb Stuart had reconnoitered. On June 25, the first day of what came to be called the Seven Days Battles, the plan of attack was set up and General John Magruder conducted operations around Oak Hill that were intended to lead McClellan to think the Confederate force was larger than it was. Did he succeed?

A. *Yes. McClellan, who had learned only the day before that Jackson's army was returning to the Richmond area, was so concerned that he sent a telegram to Secretary of War Stanton saying that the number of Confederate troops was at least 200,000. In fact, there were less than half that number. Lee fully understood the tendency of "the redoubtable Mac," as McClellan was derisively called by Confederate officers, to exaggerate the numbers opposing him, and hoped to take advantage of that weakness.*

Q. The attack against General Fitz-John Porter's isolated Union troops on the twenty-sixth was led by General A. P. Hill's division, but the attack was supposed to be supported on the flank by Stonewall Jackson. But when Jackson did not show up, Hill attacked anyway in the late afternoon and was badly beaten, suffering heavy casualties. What was the explanation for Jackson's failure to appear?

The Civil War Quiz Book

A. *This question has long puzzled historians, but it is now generally agreed that Jackson's men, and the general himself in particular, were suffering from exhaustion. Jackson was not himself throughout the whole Seven Days period.*

Q. Hill's 1,500-man losses at the Battle of Mechanicsville did not deter Lee from launching another attack on the third day, June 27. Lee was aware that McClellan had shifted his base camp and all of his supplies from White House Landing to the James River. This meant that the lost battle at Mechanicsville had turned into a strategic success for the South. How so?

A. *By moving his base camp to a position with no rail lines that could carry heavy artillery, McClellan had fundamentally given up the plan to take Richmond by siege.*

Q. The Battle of Gaines's Mill did not go well for the Confederate forces through most of the third day, however. The rather complex plan called for good coordination, timing, and the crucial support of Jackson—all of which were faulty to some degree. It was not until almost sunset that General Porter's Union line was finally broken. And the victory had its costs. How many Confederate troops were killed or wounded on June 27?

    a.   4,000
    b.   7,000
    c.   9,000

A. *The answer is c, with the highest losses among General Hill's troops, which were once again the most heavily engaged.*

Q. All of the fighting was taking place on the north side of the Chickahominy River. Why didn't the 60,000 Union soldiers on the south side attack General Magruder's 27,000 men?

A. *Magruder was succeeding beyond anyone's wildest hopes in bamboozling the Union forces into believing he had more troops than they did instead of fewer than half as many. The Confederates put on a show of aggression and strength, without actually engaging in combat, that had the Yankees totally fooled.*

Q. McClellan went into a state of shock, convinced that he had been overwhelmed by a considerably superior force. On whom did he blame the loss?

A. *Stanton, Lincoln, and anybody else in Washington who had refused to send him more troops. In fact, with double the Southern forces, he might have turned the tables despite being badly positioned. Yet, however incapable he was of mounting an attack, McClellan's organizational abilities made him very good at retreating, and he moved the Union army back with remarkable dispatch.*

Q. On June 28, there was very little action, but the Union army was making good use of the day in setting up stronger positions to the north. On June 29 and June 30 rearguard battles were fought at Savage's Station and Frayser's Farm (Glendale), but the Confederates continued to have difficulty with coordination of their forces. Jackson seemed hardly aware of what was happening, and in his exhaustion several times lay down and went to sleep while fighting raged as little as two miles away. Was Jackson ever reprimanded by Lee for his dismal performance during the Seven Days?

A. *There is no record that he was, and he subsequently recovered himself and performed brilliantly for Lee.*

Q. The final battle of the Seven Days was a charge against a very strong Union position at Malvern Hill. In his frustration, Lee ordered an attack despite misgivings, leading to another casualty list in excess of 5,000. During the entire Seven Days, Lee's army was always on the attack, McClellan's always on the defensive. Were there any battles during which Confederate losses were less than Union losses?

A. *No. Throughout the Seven Days, Confederate losses were higher, often nearly double those of the Army of the Potomac. In the end, there were 30,000 men killed or wounded in the Seven Days, with nearly 20,000 being Confederates. But the South had taken nearly 6,000 prisoners and there would be no siege of Richmond.*

Q. On July 1, Lincoln signed an economic measure. The one he had signed the previous year had never been implemented, but this one would be. What was it?

A. *A federal income tax that required payment of what now seems like the measly amount of 3 percent on incomes up to $10,000 and 5 percent over that income level. It would bring in about $55 million in the course of the rest of the war, and was fully accepted as a necessary wartime measure. After the war, it became less popular and was dropped in 1872.*

Q. General McClellan set up a new base for the Army of the Potomac at Harrison's Landing on the James River. Here, the troops had to contend with a new difficulty—disease. What percentage of the unwounded men fell ill with such diseases as malaria, dysentery, and typhoid?

A. *Almost 25 percent.*

Q. Tompkinsville, Kentucky, was captured July 9 by a Confederate cavalryman who was a citizen of that state. This raider had two regiments under his command and would cause endless trouble for the Union forces. What was his name?

A. *Colonel John Hunt Morgan, who had been born in Alabama but settled in Lexington, Kentucky, after serving in the Mexican War with the 1st Kentucky.*

Q. Lincoln came to the conclusion that having the Union generals report to Secretary of War Stanton was not working well, and that it was necessary to have a military leader in Washington itself. Whom did he appoint as General-in-Chief of the Federal army?

A. *General Henry Halleck. Despite the length of time it had taken him to get from Pittsburg Landing to Corinth, his capture of the important Mississippi city at the end of May had impressed Lincoln.*

Q. Another of the South's famous cavalry raiders, Colonel Nathan Bedford Forrest, seized Murfreesboro, Tennessee, on July 11. What was the most valuable aspect of this victory?

A. *The large amount of munitions and supplies that were captured. Forrest was made a brigadier general ten days later.*

Q. What new state was created by Congress on July 14?

A. *West Virginia. It was not admitted to the Union until June 20, 1863, however.*

Q. General Pope made a bombastic speech to the troops of his new Army of Virginia in mid-July. What comparison did he make that offended many of the soldiers?

A. *He compared the soldiers of the east unfavorably with those he had commanded in the west.*

Q. Union naval forces under Admiral David Farragut engaged in a battle with the Confederate ironclad ram *Arkansas* on the Mississippi near the mouth of the Yazoo River on July 15. At one point the *Arkansas* was actually boarded, but the ship still could not be taken. What did the crew do to prevent capture?

A. *The crew retreated belowdecks and bolted the iron hatches from within.*

Q. The Second Confiscation Act was signed by Lincoln on July 17, 1862. The act stated that slaves who came into Federal hands from outside the states of the Union would be set free. Was this act one that Lincoln had initiated?

A. *No. It was the work of the most radical anti-slavery members of Congress, and Lincoln had refused to sign it until provisions were added that involved presidential power to grant amnesty. In fact, Lincoln had proposed to Congress an act that would have compensated any state that abolished slavery. This recognition that slavery was a national problem was anathema to those in Congress who wanted to punish the South severely for its actions. It was also rejected by representatives of the border states where slavery existed as being too radical a change.*

Q. Having worked on it further, Lincoln presented a draft of his Emancipation Proclamation to his Cabinet, who were surprised but generally supportive. Secretary of State William H. Seward advised against issuing it at the time, however. Was this because he opposed it?

A. *No. He agreed with the idea that the slaves in the Confederate States should be declared free, but he felt that if the proclamation was issued so soon after McClellan's withdrawal from the area around Richmond following the Seven Days Battles, it would be taken as a sign of desperation. He advised waiting until a significant military victory had been achieved.*

Q. Lincoln was strongly impressed by Seward's reasoning and agreed to hold off the issuance of the Emancipation Proclamation. Did the delay cause him problems?

A. *Yes, because it was generally assumed that he was against freeing the slaves and agreed with the view pressed on him by General McClellan that the Confederate States should not be punished. Lincoln's position on this issue had in fact changed greatly since the beginning of the war, when he had insisted that war was necessary to preserve the Union, not to free the slaves. As the war dragged on, however, he began to believe that the freeing of the slaves in the Confederate States was a military necessity, saying, "This government cannot much longer play a game in which it stakes all, and its enemies stake nothing." But with the delay in issuing the proclamation, his changed position was not understood and the abolitionists roundly attacked him for not taking a position that he had in fact already adopted.*

Q. On August 3, the new General-in-Chief, Henry Halleck, ordered McClellan to pull his Army of the Potomac back as far as Alexandria, Virginia, in order to protect Washington. How did McClellan respond to this order?

A. *McClellan was furious. He had already said that the man appointed over him as General-in-Chief was his "inferior." But McClellan was angry with everyone, calling Secretary of War Stanton "a deformed hypocrite and villain," as James McPherson reports in* Battle Cry of Freedom. *By this time, in fact, McClellan was already in contact with Democratic politicians who wanted him to run against Lincoln in 1894.*

Q. General Nathaniel "Commissary" Banks, who had been routed by Stonewall Jackson in the Shenandoah Valley earlier in the year, thought he had a chance to get revenge by attacking Jackson's forces at Cedar Mountain, Virginia. Initially he was able to drive back a segment of Jackson's army, even though he had only half as many men. But a counterattack led by General A. P. Hill forced Banks to retreat. What percentage of Banks's forces were casualties of this battle?

A. *Banks lost 30 percent of his 6,000 men, 314 of them killed.*

Q. In mid-August, Union cavalry almost captured Jeb Stuart. He escaped but lost something in the process. What was it?

A. *His famous plumed hat was grabbed by a Union soldier. Of considerably more importance, an officer who was captured had a copy of Lee's orders, which finally made the overconfident General Pope recognize that he was seriously threatened by Lee's army. He retreated to the northern side of the Rappahannock River to await expected reinforcements from General McClellan.*

Q. Who was gravely criticized by *New York Tribune* editor Horace Greeley on August 19?

A. *President Lincoln was held up to scorn for not stating that the slaves were free. Still not ready to issue the Emancipa-*

tion Proclamation, the president replied three days later by saying that his intent was to save the Union: "If I could save the Union without freeing any slave I would do it, and if I could save it by freeing all the slaves I would do it." Greeley's editorial had been titled "The Prayer of Twenty Millions," but in fact there was mixed opinion on the subject throughout the North.

Q. Jeb Stuart made a raid on General Pope's base. What did he steal that belonged to Pope?

A. *The general's best dress-uniform coat. In addition, it became Stuart's turn to capture important documents, which revealed to Lee that McClellan's forces were expected to join Pope in two days.*

Q. Resorting to radical military strategy, General Lee divided his army, sending Jackson and his 25,000 men off to the northwest in an attempt to encircle Pope. Did Pope's forces become aware of Jackson's movement?

A. *Yes, but Pope assumed that Jackson was heading back into the Shenandoah Valley. Instead, Jackson turned and headed for Manassas Junction, the main supply depot for Pope's army, some twenty-five miles behind it. In just two days Jackson had marched his men over fifty miles, and they fell on the food at Manassas like rabbits on a lettuce patch. They were also able to refit themselves with new shoes. Taking everything they could with them, they burned what remained.*

Q. McClellan had reluctantly sent forward two corps from his army to join the despised Pope, but on the twenty-eighth

Halleck urgently requested McClellan to send a third corps. What did McClellan do?

A. *He refused, going so far as to send a communiqué to Lincoln suggesting that Pope should be left to "get out of this scrape himself." The newspapers had a name for McClellan—Mac The Unready—and Lincoln would have liked to get rid of him. However, the general's own men were extremely fond of him, and since he was blaming Lincoln and Stanton for the failure at Richmond, it was a politically difficult time to remove him from command.*

Q. Pope, meanwhile, had his cavalry frantically searching for Jackson, who had disappeared after leaving the smoking ruins of the supply depot at Manassas. How far had he gone?

A. *Only about two miles. He was sequestered on a ridge that was heavily wooded, awaiting the arrival of troops under General Longstreet.*

Q. Pope had his troops marching back and forth in one direction after another, responding to what kept turning out to be false reports about Jackson's whereabouts. Jackson moved his troops toward Groveton, Virginia, and then deliberately revealed himself by attacking troops under the command of General Rufus King. There was fierce fighting in this twilight Battle of Groveton, and Jackson's army suffered high casualties, but the results were worth it—he succeeded in drawing General Pope into battle the next morning, August 29, before the reinforcements from McClellan had arrived. What mistake did Pope make on the twenty-ninth?

A. *His troops were scattered, and instead of waiting until he had his entire force together, he kept throwing smaller forces at Jackson. They fought furiously, but were repulsed each time.*

Q. One of the corps that had been sent by McClellan to reinforce Pope was commanded by McClellan's close friend Major General Fitz-John Porter. He also loathed Pope. On the twenty-ninth, as the battle was in full fury, Pope sent orders for Porter to attack Jackson's right flank. Did Porter carry out these orders?

A. *No, because General Longstreet had arrived, and Lee placed his troops along the very side of the line that Pope had ordered Porter to attack. Made a scapegoat by Pope, Porter was court-martialed in November. He spent the next twenty years fighting to clear his name and was finally recommissioned by an act of Congress in 1886.*

Q. The next day, August 30, General Pope became convinced that the Confederates were retreating and decided to go after them. Was Pope correct that Lee's army was withdrawing?

A. *Pope was as wrong about this as he was about almost everything else at Second Bull Run. After bitter fighting, the Union troops were pushed back to Henry House, where Stonewall Jackson had made his famous stand at First Bull Run. Again they were forced from the field by Jackson, and within three days Pope's army had withdrawn all the way back to Washington. With 14,000 men killed, wounded, or taken prisoner, Second Bull Run, or Second Manassas, was an even greater disaster than First Bull Run. The Confederate casualties were also high, at 10,000, but the clear Southern victory gave hope that the Union could indeed be defeated.*

Q. Lee recognized that Washington itself was too heavily fortified to be taken, but he was determined to follow up the victory at Second Bull Run with a strike into Union territory. Into what Union state did he move his troops and why did he choose it?

A. *He moved into Maryland because it was well known that the state contained many Southern sympathizers. But Union sentiment was strong in the area around Frederick where he made camp and the reception was very far from hospitable.*

Q. Despite the misgivings of some of his Cabinet, as well as some doubts of his own, Lincoln named McClellan to take over the Union Army of Virginia. What was his reasoning?

A. *Not only was "Little Mac" beloved by the common foot soldier, he was always the best man Lincoln had at getting troops prepared for battle—even if he was reluctant to get into one. Considering the demoralized and exhausted state of so many troops following the retreat from Bull Run, McClellan still seemed the best man to restore order and confidence. Pope was dispatched to Minnesota to deal with a serious Sioux uprising. He remained Commander of the Department of the Northwest for the remainder of the war, and did his job well in this less-exposed position.*

Q. On September 9, General Lee issued his Special Order No. 191, which concerned the capture of Harpers Ferry, now in West Virginia, where there was a strong Union garrison. Into how many parts did the daring Lee divide his army this time?

A. *Four, with three separate units converging on Harpers Ferry from different directions, while the fourth marched across*

South Mountain, which lay between the Confederate base at Frederick, Maryland, and Harpers Ferry.

Q. What was found wrapped around three cigars at a recently abandoned Confederate campsite on September 13?

A. *A copy of Special Order No. 191. It was immediately conveyed to McClellan.*

Q. McClellan had been moving slowly toward Frederick with the Army of the Potomac, into which the Army of Virginia had been absorbed. With Lee's plans now in his hands, McClellan had a perfect opportunity to engage Lee's separated forces one by one. What did he do?

A. *Waited until the next morning, in typical McClellan fashion, to get moving. In the meantime, Jeb Stuart found out from one of his spies that McClellan had a copy of Lee's orders. Lee changed plans and got forces to two of the major gaps in the South Mountain range, Turner's Gap and Crampton's Gap, which the tardy Union forces had to fight their way through on the fourteenth, thus gaining Lee an entire day.*

Q. Lee himself had only 19,000 men with him and did not know how matters were going at Harpers Ferry. What did he do?

A. *Quickly retreated to the town of Sharpsburg behind Antietam Creek near the Maryland border with West Virginia. There the message came through from Stonewall Jackson that Harpers Ferry had indeed been taken, with nearly 12,000 prisoners captured.*

The Civil War Quiz Book

Q. Name the river in the upper left-hand corner of the map below showing Sharpsburg and Antietam Creek.

A. *It is the Potomac. If Lee's army were to be driven back from their position, they might easily find themselves trapped with the Potomac at their backs.*

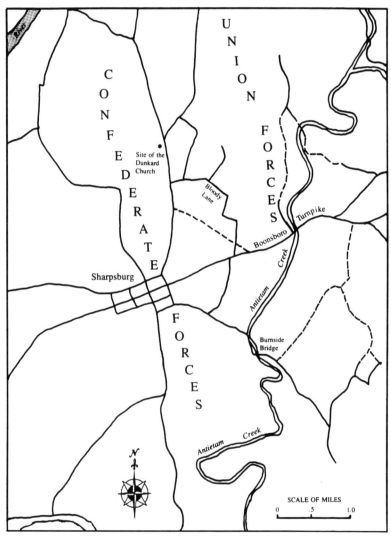

Q. If McClellan had moved fast enough, arriving at Antietam on September 16, how large a Confederate force would he have encountered?

    a. 19,000
    b. 30,000
    c. 35,000

A. *The answer is b, a force consisting of Lee's 19,000 and about half of Jackson's men, who had already arrived. McClellan had 60,000 with another 15,000 closer to the scene than the three Confederate divisions still marching toward Antietam.*

Q. The battle of Antietam, or of Sharpsburg, as Southerners call it, began at dawn on September 17 with an attack by the three divisions under General Hooker on the Confederate divisions commanded by General John B. Hood and General Jubal A. Early. How many separate attacks would the Union army launch in the course of the day?

A. *Five, which was one of the main reasons the Confederate forces were not destroyed, as Lincoln had told McClellan to make every effort to do. McClellan botched it through bad coordination of his forces. The first assault lasted an hour and, with heavy losses on both sides, left the Southern line about where it had been at the start, although it had been pushed back for a time. A second assault left the commander of these fresh forces, General Joseph Mansfield, mortally wounded, and although his troops pushed the Confederate forces of Hood and Early back to Dunkard Church, they could press no farther.*

Q. A third attack by a single division also failed to break the line at Dunkard Church. It was stopped by the arrival of two more Confederate divisions. What were they allowed to do for an hour after their arrival on the battle site?

A. *Rest. They had marched all night to get there.*

Q. What was the Bloody Lane?

A. *This was a sunken road at the center of the Confederate line where the most horrific fighting of the day took place. Two Union divisions pressed forward under extremely heavy fire until they reached the high ground near the present site of the large stone Observation Tower. From there, they were able to dominate the whole rebel line along the sunken road. But an additional charge that probably would have finished Lee's forces was not mounted.*

Q. Why might the outcome also have been different if a Union general had been willing to get his feet wet?

A. *General Ambrose Burnside wasted several hours trying to get his men over Stone Bridge (renamed Burnside Bridge) over Antietam Creek, when it could easily have been forded at several points. By the time he did get across, the Confederates had largely withdrawn to the surrounding hills. No one knows why Burnside became so fixated on taking the bridge, but it was just one more inexplicable misjudgment in a day of blunders that might otherwise have brought an early end to the war.*

Q. On September 18, many of Lee's commanders urged an immediate retreat. Did he follow that advice?

A. *No. He believed that he knew McClellan completely, and that the Union general would not launch a new attack. For the morale of his army, he wanted to wait twenty-four hours before making a withdrawal, so that it could continue to be said that the Army of Northern Virginia had never been driven from the field. He was absolutely correct about the behavior of McClellan who took one look at the casualties suffered, wired Washington that he had achieved a great victory, and ignored Lincoln's charge to destroy Lee's army.*

Q. Which side suffered the greatest casualties at Antietam?

A. *The losses in what is often called the bloodiest day of the Civil War were appalling on both sides, but the Confederate losses were greater, with about 700 more dead than the 2,000 on the Union side, and almost three times as many missing. Only the Union number of wounded was greater, by about 500, for a horrifying total of 9,500.*

Q. Given the losses, and the failure to destroy Lee's army, Antietam became a strategic rather than a total victory. It did stop the invasion of Maryland, and put the South in a defensive posture once again. Perhaps equally important, it gave Lincoln the excuse he needed to do what?

A. *Make public the Emancipation Proclamation, to take effect on January 1, 1863, declaring the slaves freed as of that date in all rebel states. Loyal states retained the right to keep slaves.*

Q. In what foreign country did the Emancipation Proclamation have a particularly positive effect in respect to the Union cause?

A. *Great Britain. Jefferson Davis had hoped from the outset that he could enlist the aid of Great Britain for the Confed-*

eracy. And indeed, both in the British government and among the British people, there was considerable sentiment for such a move. But the defeat at Antietam raised new questions bout the Confederacy's ability to survive, and the Emancipation Proclamation finally transformed the war, in British eyes, into a war for freedom.

Q. On October 2, Confederate general Earl Van Dorn tried to retake what crucial railroad center that General Halleck had taken at the end of May?

A. *Corinth, Mississippi. Fighting in the area lasted for four days, but the Union forces under General William Rosecrans held firm and very nearly captured the entire Confederate attack force. As it was, more than 1,700 Confederate troops were reported missing, with nearly 2,500 killed or wounded. The Union losses were a few hundred less in terms of casualties, and almost eight times less in terms of men listed as missing.*

Q. On the eighth of October, another battle of even larger dimensions in respect to casualties occurred at Perryville, Kentucky. Which side prevailed there?

A. *General Don Carlos Buell's Union troops, more than twice the strength of General Braxton Bragg's Confederates, carried the day, but Union losses were greater in every category.*

Q. Name the Confederate general who for a second time made an embarrassing foray against the forces of General McClellan.

A. *Over a period of several days beginning on October 9, Jeb Stuart made his Second Ride Around McClellan. General*

Lee had ordered a repeat of Stuart's stunt for the express purpose of embarrassing McClellan—hoping to further stir up the demands of Northern Peace Democrats, already enraged by the Emancipation Proclamation, to end the war.

Q. On October 10, Jefferson Davis issued a controversial call for the drafting of 4,500 men. In what did the controversy lie?

A. *He called for the drafting of slaves to help construct fortifications around Richmond. This request was made in part to offset another controversial step, an amendment to the draft law that exempted from service those who owned more than twenty slaves. There was a great deal of resentment about the latter among less affluent Southerners who bore the brunt of the fighting. The idea of drafting slaves was intended to show that those exempted would have to pay a price, too.*

Q. Why did Lincoln relieve General Don Carlos Buell of his command of Union forces in Kentucky and Tennessee on October 24?

A. *Because Buell had been unable to prevent General Bragg from getting his remaining troops out of Kentucky. Lincoln's impatience with generals who didn't follow through and capture defeated Confederate forces was growing. General Rosecrans was given the additional charge of commanding these troops.*

Q. To whom did Lincoln in late October send a telegram with a caustic inquiry concerning fatigued horses that hadn't done anything since Antietam?

A. *General McClellan, who had come up with a new excuse for doing nothing: "sore tongued and fatigued horses." Lincoln's sarcasm apparently had its intended effect, since McClellan proceeded to at least get his army moving across the Potomac into Virginia.*

Q. Lincoln's fellow Republicans had been deeply afraid that the announcement of the Emancipation Proclamation would cause heavy political losses in the November 4 state and congressional elections. Were Democratic gains in fact very great?

A. *On the surface they seemed significant. The election of Democratic governors in both New York and New Jersey, states that were extremely important to the war effort in terms of both manpower and supplies, were particularly stunning. The legislatures in New Jersey as well as Illinois and Indiana changed hands, and thirty-four seats were gained in Congress. But historian James M. McPherson has challenged the prevailing view that the elections were a triumph for the Democrats. He has pointed out that the Republicans actually gained five Senate seats, and the losses in the House were smaller than usual in nonpresidential election years. Even where the Democrats prevailed, the margins were often slim. Anti-abolition voices in the 1860s were the loudest ones around, but their support was not as strong as the noise they made.*

Q. On the day after the election, Lincoln took a step that he had been considering, and that others had urged upon him for some time. What was this major step?

A. *He relieved General McClellan of his command. The fact that he made this decision when he did provides significant insight into the complexity of Lincoln's character as a man and as a politician. Lincoln had been snubbed, abused, and disobeyed by McClellan almost from the start. A lesser man would certainly have dispensed with McClellan's service far sooner. But Lincoln recognized that there was no one better at turning raw recruits, many of them urban men who had never had a gun in their hands, into soldiers. He had stuck with him, despite his dislike and his increasing frustration with McClellan's failures in the field, because he recognized and genuinely admired the one genius that McClellan had, for training and organizing an army. But by the end of 1862, that army was in itself experienced. Fort Donelson, Shiloh, Island Number Ten, Corinth, the Seven Days, Second Bull Run/Manassas, Antietam—on all fronts, under all commands, there was now an army of experienced survivors. McClellan's one great talent was no longer needed, and his great faults as a field commander could no longer be tolerated. The political slyness that was also part of Lincoln's makeup is also evident in the timing of his action. McClellan was an anti-abolitionist and a very likely contender against Lincoln for the presidency two years later. By firing McClellan the day after the Republicans had survived the bombast of the anti-abolitionist Democrats, it sent a strong message and must have given Lincoln a sweet moment of revenge for all the invective he had taken from the general.*

Q. When General McClellan received notice two days later of his removal, he was stunned. He returned to his home in Trenton, New Jersey, where he waited for his next appointment, but it was never forthcoming. Whom did Lincoln appoint in his stead as general of the Army of the Potomac?

A. *Major General Ambrose Burnside, despite his peculiar be-havior at Antietam. Burnside had twice turned down this command before, feeling himself unqualified for the job. But he decided that he could not refuse what was couched as an order.*

Q. General Burnside decided to march again on Richmond, but by a different route, crossing the Rappahannock River at Fredericksburg, Virginia, and then driving south to Richmond. He moved his 110,000-man army with dispatch to Falmouth, across the river from Fredericksburg, arriving there in the first week of December. But the army had to wait there for almost a week because some crucial equipment had gone astray. What was this equipment?

A. *Pontoon bridges. The river was too deep to be forded. Burnside's orders concerning the bridges had been unclear—a failing that always plagued him.*

Q. By the time the pontoons arrived, Lee's 78,000-man army was dug in on the other side of the river, with General Longstreet's corps holding a four-mile-long stretch of hills above open ground that the invading army would have to cross. Jackson's troops were ranged along a less commanding wooded ridge on the right flank of the Confederate line. Because sharpshooters in Fredericksburg were able to pick off the Union engineers when they started laying the pontoons on December 11, it was necessary to ferry soldiers across to take the town, which had been largely evacuated of civilians. Thus it was not until the morning of the thirteenth that Burnside's forces were across the river and ready to attack. Despite the lost time, the weather gave the Union troops an early advantage. What was it?

A. *There was a dense fog that morning and the Confederate forces were not able to see what was happening until the Union troops were almost upon them.*

Q. A division under the command of Major General George Gordon Meade managed to penetrate the Confederate line after Jackson's artillery had been bested by Union guns. How quickly did Major General William Franklin back up Meade's men with the 50,000 troops under him?

A. *He didn't send them in. Once again, General Burnside's confusing orders, and a last-minute change in plan, kept the Union army from exploiting a breakthrough. The Confederate line was re-formed by reinforcements.*

Q. At the other end of the Confederate line, the steep rise called Marye's Heights was the focus of repeated Union charges. How many charges were made at Marye's Heights that day?

A. *Fourteen, all of them fruitless. The bravery of the Union troops was extraordinary, the casualties appalling. In the end there were almost 13,000 Union casualties. The defending Confederate line had just over 5,000 casualties. Fredericksburg was a disaster for the Union army, and two nights later Burnside retreated to the north side of the Rappahannock. He then issued a statement taking total responsibility for the debacle at Fredericksburg.*

Q. Near the end of 1862, Union colonel Thomas W. Higginson wrote in his diary at Camp Saxton, near Beaufort, South Carolina, ''It takes only a few days to see the absurdity of doubting the military promise of these men.'' Who were the men he referred to?

A. *The 1st Carolina Volunteers, a regiment of black troops led by white officers. This was the first such regiment formed during the Civil War. Higginson commanded them until a combat wound forced his retirement in May of 1864.*

Q. During December of 1862, General Grant was leading a force overland toward Vicksburg, Mississippi, the capture of which was essential to complete Union control of the Mississippi River. But he was forced to turn back because of General Earl Van Dorn's raid on his supply depot at Holly Springs, Mississippi, and the continual harassment of his supply and communications lines by the Army of Tennessee cavalry brigade led by the brilliant Brigadier General Nathan Bedford Forrest. How much formal training had Forrest had as a cavalry officer?

A. *None. The forty-one-year-old Forrest had accumulated a fortune as a slave trader and plantation owner before the war. He put his wealth at $1.5 million and used his fortune to help equip his troops. He was a great general but an often disliked man, even in the South. After the war he became one of the founders of the Ku Klux Klan.*

Q. On the seventeenth of December, Senate Republicans held the second caucus in two days to discuss problems between Secretary of the Treasury Salmon Chase and Secretary of State William Seward. Which secretary was the chief troublemaker in this instance?

A. *Salmon Chase, who had been complaining that Seward was influencing Lincoln to move slowly on controversial abolitionist issues. Chase was a radical on slavery issues and felt Lincoln was not moving fast enough even with the announcement of the Emancipation Proclamation. Both men ended up offering their resignations to the president, but Lincoln finessed the problem with some complex political maneuvering and managed to keep both Chase and Seward in office.*

Q. Trying to put a stop to the illegal trading in cotton between the South and some Northern speculators, what people did General Grant single out as a "class" in his highly controversial General Order No. 11?

A. *Jews. It was true that several Jews were among the most flagrant speculators, but it quite naturally caused an uproar and Lincoln rescinded it in early January.*

Q. What military governor of a Union-held Southern city did Jefferson Davis call a felon and an enemy of mankind in the fourth week of December?

A. *General Benjamin Butler, whose iron-heel treatment of the citizens of New Orleans continued to cause fury among Confederates. Davis went so far as to call for Butler's immediate execution if he were to be captured.*

Q. Although General Grant had been prevented from getting to Vicksburg by the exploits of Generals Forrest and Van Dorn, General Sherman had brought another force, which was supposed to link up with Grant's, to a point north of Vicksburg. Why didn't Sherman know that Grant had pulled back?

A. *Because Forrest had destroyed fifty miles of both railroads and telegraph lines. Sherman attacked the Confederate po-*

sition at Chickasaw Bayou, but even though he had a larger force his men were thrown back by the deeply entrenched Confederates on December 29, with the Union soldiers suffering nearly four times as many fatalities and having ten times as many wounded or missing.

Q. The U.S.S. *Rhode Island* managed to rescue forty-seven men on December 30 as what famous ship foundered in a storm and went down off Cape Hatteras?

A. *The* Monitor, *like its famous antagonist, the* Merrimac *(later the* Virginia*), met an ignominious end. Sixteen men and officers died.*

Q. On December 30, 42,000 troops of the Army of the Cumberland under General Rosecrans arrived at Murfreesboro, Tennessee, which had been held by Confederate forces since mid-July. On the eve of the battle against General Bragg's army, soldiers on both sides joined in singing "Home, Sweet Home" together. Is this true or false?

A. *It is true. Bands traveled with many regiments on both sides throughout the war, though more commonly with Union forces. On this particular December night, there were bands present on both sides. The armies were encamped close enough to hear one another's music. What began as a musical contest to drown out one another with "Yankee Doodle Dandy" versus "Dixie" and other songs, ended with the plaintive sounds of "Home, Sweet Home" rising through the darkness.*

Q. The battle of Stones River or Murfreesboro began at dawn the next day with a ferocious Confederate attack. There were heavy losses on both sides during the long day. That night, which commander wired his government seat that he had won a great victory?

A. *General Bragg wired Richmond, believing that Rosecrans was preparing to pull back. But when the sun came up on the first day of 1863, Rosecrans was still very much there.*

Part Four
1863

Q. In what country were the following words composed by the citizens of a large manufacturing center in response to the formal issuing of the Emancipation Proclamation on January 1, 1863? : "We honor your Free States, as a singularly happy abode for the working millions where industry is honored. Since we have discerned . . . that the victory of the free North . . . will strike off the fetters of the slave, you have attracted our warm and earnest sympathy."

A. *These words were part of a letter drawn up by the citizens of Manchester, England, and sent to President Lincoln. With the change in public opinion this letter demonstrates, there was now a much lessened possibility of Great Britain aiding the Confederacy.*

Q. Which of the following several states did the Emancipation Proclamation *not* apply to, and why not?

a. Texas
b. Florida
c. Tennessee
d. Arkansas

A. *The answer is* c. *Tennessee, which had seceded, was exempt because it was almost entirely in Union hands. The same was true for southern Louisiana, parts of Virginia that were occupied, Missouri and Kentucky, which had ultimately not seceded, and the new state of West Virginia. Thus the Emancipation Proclamation affected only those areas where it could not at the time be put into effect—the core of the Confederacy. This was one reason why radical abolitionists thought it did not go nearly far enough. But the Proclamation succeeded as a statement of intention, and had wide psychological effects.*

Q. At Stones River, or Murfreesboro, General John C. Breckinridge's division made an attack on a ridge held by Union forces that led to the loss of 1,500 Confederate troops in a single hour. Was he blamed for this disaster?

A. *No. It had been ordered by General Bragg. Breckinridge, who had been vice-president under James Buchanan and come in second to Lincoln in the 1860 election in terms of electoral votes as the Southern Democratic candidate, was a man of independent mind. He had told Bragg that the attack would fail, because even if they took the ridge, his troops would then be exposed to Union artillery. He was exactly right. His command in disarray, Bragg then withdrew twenty-five miles south on January 3.*

Q. On January 11, Fort Hindman, Arkansas, fell to the Union general John Alexander McClernand with the help of gunboats under Admiral David Porter, which bombarded the fort from the Arkansas River. Nearly 4,800 Confederate prisoners were taken, but General Grant initially termed this success ''a wild goose chase.'' Why?

A. *Grant had not authorized it and initially thought that McClernand was acting on his own hook, which he was prone to do. In late 1862 he had been busy politicking in Washington, trying to get command of the taking of Vicksburg away from Grant. In the Fort Hindman incident, it turned out that Grant's protégé, General Sherman, had suggested the attack. But Grant would have more trouble with this self-congratulatory upstart later on.*

Q. On January 15, the Confederate privateer *Florida* managed to evade the Union blockade at Mobile, Alabama. How many Union ships and merchant ships supplying the North did the *Florida* capture in the next eighteen months?

    a.   29
    b.   37
    c.   69

A. *The answer is b, second only to the record of the Alabama, which had sunk a Union ship in the waters off Texas only four days earlier, and would cause havoc on sea-lanes around the world and take a total of sixty-nine prizes.*

Q. General Burnside had marched the Army of the Potomac to the banks of the Rappahannock with the intention of making a new assault on Fredericksburg. By the twenty-second he had to give up the effort and start pulling his forces back because of something that had been happening for a day and a half. What was it?

A. *It had been raining nonstop. The terrain was nothing but mud and the river itself was badly swollen.*

Q. In his frustration, General Burnside relieved Generals Joseph Hooker, William B. Franklin, William T. H. Brooks, and John Newton of their Army of the Potomac commands. What was Lincoln's response to this step?

A. *After conferring with Burnside, General Halleck, and his Cabinet, Lincoln rescinded Burnside's order, accepted Burnside's offer to resign, and replaced him with General Hooker. Burnside himself was assigned to the Department of the Ohio, apparently much to his own relief.*

Q. In late January, General Grant ordered that efforts be resumed to construct what in the marshes opposite Vicksburg?

A. *A canal. The hope was to repeat the success of the canal at Island Number Ten the previous year. But these wetlands were too swampy, and defeated the effort at every turn.*

Q. What foreign government's offer of mediation between North and South was officially rejected on February 6, 1863?

A. *The French government, under Napoleon III. Only two days earlier Queen Victoria had stated that Great Britain would not attempt to mediate because it was not believed that such efforts could lead to any success. In fact, Great Britain was beginning to hope that the North would win, but hedging its bets.*

Q. In mid-February the U.S. Senate enacted a law similar to one that the Confederate Congress had passed the previous April. What did it put into effect?

A. *Conscription, the drafting of men to replace the dwindling numbers of volunteers. Both the North and the South also had serious problems of desertion. The figures on both sides for those "missing" after major battles often included as many deserters as prisoners.*

Q. In the aftermath of Stones River, General Leonidas Polk and General William J. Hardee asked Jefferson Davis to replace

General Bragg with General Joseph Johnston as commander of the Army of Tennessee. What book had Hardee published in 1855 that caused his views to be given extra weight?

A. *This former commandant of cadets at West Point was the author of* Rifle and Light Infantry Tactics, *a modernization of Napoleon's methods that were used by both sides in the Civil War. In this instance, though, Davis left Bragg in place.*

Q. On February 28, the U.S.S. *Montauk,* even though under fire from shore artillery, was able to shell and set on fire the Confederate privateer *Nashville.* The *Montauk* was commanded by a commodore who had been commended by Congress on February 3 for his service as captain of what ship?

A. *Commodore J. L. Worden had been the commander of the* Merrimack. *The* Montauk *was also an ironclad, and this engagement on the Ogeechee River in Georgia once again proved that ironclads, whatever their problems at sea, were highly effective in the calmer waters of rivers.*

Q. The Enrollment Act, authorizing a draft, was passed by the full Congress on March 3. By the end of 1864, 170,000 men had been drafted. How many of those who were drafted hired substitutes to fight for them?

A. *Around 120,000 paid $300 to poor rural and urban young men to fight in their stead.*

Q. In one of Colonel John S. Mosby's daring and infuriating raids, the Confederate hero captured Union General E. H. Stoughton at Fairfax Court House, Virginia, which he had made his temporary headquarters. Also captured was one of Stoughton's subordinates, Colonel D. H. Dulang. This involved a strained reunion of a kind most common to civil wars. How so?

A. *One of Mosby's raiders was Colonel Dulang's son, French.*

Q. An explosion at the Confederate Ordnance Laboratory near Richmond killed or injured sixty-nine people on March 13. How many of them were women?

   a. 17
   b. 38
   c. 63

A. *The answer is c. The employment of large numbers of women in factories in the South was a consequence of Confederate manpower shortages, prefiguring what would happen in World War I and World War II.*

Q. In mid-March of 1863, there were two admirals trying to converge on Vicksburg—one, David Farragut, trying to move up the Mississippi from below, the other, David Porter, trying to reach it from above. What was the unusual relationship of these two Union admirals?

A. *They were adoptive brothers. David Farragut had served under David Porter's father in the war of 1812, and the senior Porter had given him his first command, as master of a prize ship, when he was only twelve, the same year the younger Porter was born.*

Q. Admiral Porter controlled the Mississippi above Vicksburg and Admiral Farragut controlled it from below Port Hudson to the Gulf. But that left a two hundred-mile stretch between Vicksburg and Port Hudson that was under Confederate control. Since the Red River converged with the Mississippi between the two points, the Confederates were able to supply both bluff towns from Louisiana. Farragut decided it was imperative to run past Port Hudson, which was heavily armed. He sailed north with seven ships. How many actually got past Port Hudson on March 14?

A. *Only two, including Farragut's own flagship, the* Hartford. *The once-great steamer* Mississippi *was sunk, and Farragut termed the exercise a disaster. But Admiral Porter regarded it as a "godsend" that the two ships had gotten through, and General Grant, who was trying to reach Vicksburg overland on a route parallel with Porter's, agreed. They were correct, and Farragut later revised his opinion, seeing the dash past Port Hudson as his greatest success except for the capture of New Orleans.*

Q. Beginning on March 16, Admiral Porter tried to wend his way with a fleet of ironclads through the bayous north of Vicksburg, but after five days was forced to give up the effort. In retreating, it was necessary to steam backward for one hundred miles. Why?

A. *The channels were so narrow that it was impossible to turn around.*

Q. "The colored population is the great *available,* and yet unavailed of, force for restoring the Union. The bare sight of fifty thousand armed and drilled black soldiers on the banks of the Mississippi would end the rebellion at once." To what border-state governor did Lincoln write these words at the end of March?

A. *Tennessee's governor, Andrew Johnson, who would become Lincoln's running mate in 1864.*

Q. On April 2 in Richmond, Jefferson Davis climbed onto a cart, threw some coins on the ground to gain attention, and then began to speak to about a thousand people. What was he trying to achieve?

A. *He was trying to persuade the mob that had instigated a bread riot to return home. Food was in extremely short supply in Richmond. Even Lee's army outside the city was on half rations. The mob, which was made up almost entirely of women, first demanded bread, but then began seizing clothing and other items from stores. The militia had been called to quell the riot, but the mob ignored it. Davis gave them five minutes to disperse or face fire from the militia, and after more than four minutes and a second warning, they turned and left.*

Q. Admiral Samuel F. du Pont, against his better judgment, tried to capture Charleston, South Carolina, on April 7 with a fleet of nine ironclads. Why were the buoys in the harbor of particular help to the Confederate soldiers that fired on the ironclads from Fort Sumter and Fort Moultrie?

A. *Because each time an ironclad sailed past a buoy the artillery gunners in the forts could tell exactly how far away the ship was. As a result, one damaged ironclad sank the following day and the rest had slunk out of the harbor within two hours, all of them damaged.*

Q. As a partial result of the Richmond bread riot, Jefferson Davis exhorted his compatriots to give far more land over to the growing of food and less to what two crops?

A. *Cotton and tobacco, the major cash crops. The big planta-*
tion owners were reluctant to do this, particularly in respect
to cotton, which was selling for six times what it had brought
before the war. Many Northern merchants continued to buy
cotton from the South while both the Union and Confederate
governments looked the other way.

Q. General Grant and Admiral Porter had agreed on a new plan
to take Vicksburg. Grant would take his troops down the
western bank of the Mississippi, and then cross over to the
eastern bank some twenty-five miles south of Vicksburg.
What did this plan require Porter to do?

A. *It meant that he would have to get some of his ships past*
Vicksburg to act as ferries for Grant's troops as well as to
bring supplies. He achieved this feat, under heavy bombard-
ment, on the night of April 16–17, losing only one of twelve
ships, and got eleven out of eighteen supply ships through a
week later.

Q. What was the special importance of the ride made by three
cavalry regiments under Colonel Benjamin Henry Grierson,
beginning in mid-April, from La Grange, Tennessee, to Baton Rouge, Louisiana?

A. *This brilliant ride was undertaken in order to distract Con-*
federate troops from Grant's crossing below Vicksburg, and
to tie up as many Confederate troops as possible to keep
them from the Vicksburg area. The great success of Grier-
son's Ride, as it came to be known, led to his elevation to the
rank of brigadier general in June 1863.

Q. What law passed by the Confederate Congress in the last
week of April was labeled ''confiscatory'' by some citizens?

A. *A graduated income tax. Other taxes on food and clothing were more acceptable.*

Q. At the end of April 1863, General Lee's army at Fredericksburg consisted of 60,000 men. How much larger was General Hooker's Army of the Potomac?

A. *At 134,000 men, it was more than twice as large. This permitted Hooker to adopt one of Lee's own strategies, dividing his army into two parts. Hooker's force of 70,000 made a march to the west, planning to turn and attack Lee on one flank while a smaller force of 30,000 under the command of General John Sedgwick moved in south of Fredericksburg on Lee's other flank. The remaining troops were kept back, ready to move in whichever direction they were needed.*

Q. The flanking movement began on April 27, and by April 29, Hooker joined his men at Chancellorsville, ten miles to the northwest of Fredericksburg. It appeared that he had Lee right where he wanted him, ready to be hemmed in from both sides. What crucial mistake did Hooker then make?

A. *As so many Union generals had done before him, he halted overnight. No one yet seemed to have learned the lesson about how fast Lee and Jackson could move.*

Q. As soon as he heard about the flanking march Hooker was making, on April 29, Lee sent General Richard H. Anderson out to the left with a partial division. Word was sent back that a very large Union army was gathered near Chancellorsville. Did Lee pull Anderson back?

A. *Most generals would have, but not Lee. He sent out a division under General Lafayette McLaws to joint Anderson at midnight on the thirtieth.*

Q. Stonewall Jackson then followed McLaws at dawn with three more divisions, leaving only one division to defend Fredericksburg against the Union force under command of General Sedgwick. As soon as he reached Chancellorsville, Jackson did something that astonished and confused General Hooker. What was it?

A. *Jackson ordered an immediate attack. Hooker couldn't believe what was happening, since he fully expected to destroy Lee's army that day. Over the protests of his officers, Hooker ordered a retreat.*

Q. Lee and Jackson decided to take advantage of Hooker's apparent lack of nerve, and on the morning of May 2, Jackson took his three divisions on a daylong march around the Union forces to their rear. Lee was left with only 20,000 men to keep Hooker occupied. How soon did Hooker attack?

A. *He didn't. Instead, he called for one of Sedgwick's two divisions to reinforce him.*

Q. Jackson and Lee started coordinated attacks just after five o'clock, but darkness came too soon for real headway to be achieved. As Jackson was riding in front of his line, a shot wounded him in the left arm. Where did the shot come from?

A. *In the darkness he had been fired on by his own men. General Hill had also been wounded that day and Jeb Stuart took command.*

Q. Around midnight, Hooker sent a message to General Sedgwick to attack General Jubal Early's line at Fredericksburg, break through and move up on the rear of Lee's army. This meant attacking the same Marye's Heights where the Confederates had held off fourteen separate attacks in mid-December. How many charges did the Union troops make this time?

A. *Only three. The Union troops were bloodily repulsed twice, but Jubal Early's men were too few in number to hold out for long, and a bayonet charge broke through on the third try. Sedgwick then moved forward toward the rear of Lee's army, but Lee turned General McLaws's division around and it stopped Sedgwick at Salem Church.*

Q. On May 4, reinforcements from General Anderson's division and the remnants of General Early's battered force (1,000 of them had been taken prisoner) succeeded in driving General Sedgwick back toward the Rappahannock River. Sedgwick was prepared to hang on, but changed his mind. Why?

A. *It became clear that Hooker was going to retreat across the river, so Sedgwick did the same.*

Q. The victory at Chancellorsville was perhaps Lee and Jackson's greatest triumph. But it came at great cost, with the loss of 13,000 men, 1,665 of them killed. For the North it was even worse, with 17,000 losses, including 1,606 dead. Who spoke the following words in reaction to the Union defeat: "Lost, lost, all is lost"?

a. President Lincoln
b. Massachusetts senator Charles Sumner
c. Secretary of War Edwin Stanton

A. *These were the words of the Radical Republican abolitionist Charles Sumner, whose strong views had actually led a*

South Carolina congressman, Preston Brooks, to severely beat him with a cane in the congressional chamber in 1856. Lincoln's own response on learning of the utter disaster at Chancellorsville was "My God, my God! What will the country say?"

Q. On March 7, General Earl Van Dorn, who had fought on the losing side at Pea Ridge and Corinth but who had managed to defend Vicksburg against attack in the summer of 1862, died of a gunshot wound received four days earlier. In what kind of engagement had he been wounded?

A. *A notorious womanizer, Van Dorn was shot by an enraged husband, a Dr. George B. Peters.*

Q. In a further attempt to deal with manpower problems, Lincoln made what kind of proclamation on March 10?

A. *A proclamation of general amnesty. Any soldier who was absent without leave would not be charged if he returned by the first of April.*

Q. Union regiments under the command of Colonel Thomas Higginson, whose abilities he had extolled in his diary four months earlier, occupied Jacksonville, Florida, on March 10. What made these troops special?

A. *They were largely made up of black soldiers from South Carolina.*

Q. The dying man said, "Order A. P. Hill to prepare for action—pass the infantry to the front rapidly—tell Major Hawks . . ." Then he stopped and began again, "No, no, let us pass over the river and rest under the shade of the trees.'' Whose last words were these?

A. *They were the last words spoken by the deeply religious General Stonewall Jackson. The wound he received from his own men at Chancellorsville on May 2 had festered, necessitating the amputation of his left arm. Pneumonia had then set in and Jackson died at the age of thirty-nine on May 10, 1863, his death mourned in the South more than that of any other Confederate hero.*

Q. The death of Jackson only added to the worry Jefferson Davis was consumed with. What was he so worried about?

A. *The defense of Vicksburg. After three failed attempts to reach Vicksburg, followed by calls for Grant's removal that Lincoln wisely ignored, Grant's daring plan to cross south of the city with the help of Admiral Porter's fleet had succeeded. On April 30, two corps under the command of General John McClernand and General James McPherson had crossed the river. The next day they easily defeated two Confederate brigades at Port Gibson, thirty miles south of Vicksburg.*

Q. The corps under General Sherman had been left north of Vicksburg in order to distract from Grant's crossing to the south. Once that was accomplished, Sherman was able to join the rest of the army in a week, marching across the terrain on the west bank that had been prepared by McClernand's and McPherson's troops over the course of a month. With Sherman's corps now present, the Union forces amounted to 50,000. General John Pemberton, a Northern-born officer who had married a Virginian, had only 31,000 under his command at Vicksburg. What crucial mistake did he make in deploying these forces in the first week of May?

A. *He strung them out over a forty-mile line from Vicksburg due east to Jackson, Mississippi. As a result, Grant's army was able to defeat smaller Confederate forces in a series of skirmishes and battles over a period of five days, from May 12–17. A hard-fought battle at Champion's Hill, or Baker's Creek, twenty miles east of Vicksburg, proved decisive on May 16. Pemberton's troops were pushed back into Vicksburg, and Grant now controlled the supply line for the city. A siege was now possible.*

Q. Did Grant immediately decide on a siege, or did he first attempt to take the city by force?

A. *Two attacks were made, on May 19 and May 22, but the Confederates were too well entrenched for the frontal assaults to succeed. A siege was clearly the answer.*

Q. At another crucial point farther south, another siege was beginning, with Union troops commanded by General Nathaniel Banks. Where was this other siege?

A. *At Port Hudson, Louisiana. If both Vicksburg and Port Hudson fell, the Union would control the entire length of the Mississippi, cutting the Confederacy in half.*

Q. On May 25, President Lincoln rescinded the prison sentence of former Ohio congressman Clement Vallandigham. Why had he been sent to prison in the first place?

A. *Clement Laird Vallandigham was the unofficial leader of the "Copperheads," the most extreme group of Northern Peace Democrats opposed to the war. He had lost his congressional seat in 1862, but declared himself a candidate for governor of Ohio in 1863. In his speeches he attacked Lin-*

coln and his administration with such vitriolic statements that the recently appointed Commander of the Department of Ohio, General Burnside, had him arrested on the grounds that he had violated an order Burnside had issued against disloyal speech. He was convicted by a military court, which caused an uproar even among some who detested Vallandigham. In commuting his sentence, Lincoln ordered that Vallandigham be escorted to Confederate lines. He was made none too welcome in the South and went to Canada in July. From there he ran his campaign for governor, and was actually nominated by the Democrats, but soundly defeated in the fall.

Q. The first officially recognized regiment of its kind departed from Boston, Massachusetts, for South Carolina at the end of May. It would go on to legendary fame. What number was assigned to this unit?

A. *The Massachusetts 54th, commanded by twenty-three-year-old Colonel Robert Gould Shaw, whose family were prominent abolitionists, was the first officially recognized black regiment, which became the subject of the Oscar-winning film* Glory. *The South Carolina Colored Volunteers commanded by Thomas Higginson were formed earlier but were not given official War Department status as United States troops until February of 1864.*

Q. On June 3, General Lee, with two of his three corps, those under Generals James Longstreet and Richard Ewell, moved out of the Fredericksburg area. General A. P. Hill and his corps remained behind for the time being. What was General Lee's intention?

A. *He had decided once again to invade the North. In part, he once again hoped that a successful invasion would turn the*

*North against the war, but he also hoped to be able to gather
badly needed supplies.*

Q. As Lee moved his army northwest to Culpepper Court
House, Virginia, what did General Hooker want to do?

A. *He wanted to attack the remaining corps at Fredericksburg
and then drive on toward Richmond. A battle at Franklin's
Crossing near Fredericksburg on June 5, between a reconnaissance corps from the Army of the Potomac and dug-in
Confederates, made it clear that Fredericksburg was not to
be taken that easily. But Lincoln had already decided that
the Army of the Potomac should move against Lee's forces
if they attempted to invade the North. He felt Lee was taking
a big risk and could be defeated this time around.*

Q. On June 9, the biggest cavalry battle of the entire war took
place at Brandy Station a few miles north of Fredericksburg,
where Jeb Stuart was encamped. Again, the Union force was
out on reconnaissance. Why was Stuart criticized in the
Confederate press even though he finally managed to hold
his position?

A. *Because the Union cavalry, under command of General Alfred Pleasonton, initially took Stuart and his men by surprise. The dashing Stuart was greatly admired and
celebrated, but there had always been people who thought
he was a showoff, and that feeling had spread after the death
of Stonewall Jackson, who slouched around looking like an
unmade bed and seemed to have almost no interest in his
own fame.*

Q. During the last two weeks of June, as Lee moved his army
north through Maryland and into Virginia, what did General
Hooker and the Army of the Potomac do?

A. *At Lincoln's urging, Hooker turned his army away from Fredericksburg, moving north on a parallel route to the east of Lee but keeping his army between Lee and Washington. The two great armies were about thirty miles apart during much of this period, but moved closer to each other as the month wore on, and were only a little more than twenty miles apart as they moved nearer to Gettysburg.*

Q. At the same time, on the Mississippi, General Banks launched an attack on Port Hudson when the Confederates refused to surrender, but he was repulsed and had to settle in for a siege. The siege of Vicksburg continued, with a steady barrage of the town by the Union forces. Where did many of the citizens of Vicksburg take refuge during this bombardment?

A. *In caves in the hills around Vicksburg.*

Q. At Vicksburg, General McClernand stirred up trouble again by telling newspaper reporters that his troops were superior to those of Sherman and McPherson, and that if he had been properly supported on May 22, the attack would have succeeded. What did Grant do when he learned of these newspaper reports?

A. *He relieved McClernand of his command and replaced him with General Edward O. C. Ord. Many officers felt Grant had been too patient with the troublesome McClernand and were happy to be rid of him.*

Q. What was the importance of General Rosecrans's actions against Confederate forces under General Bragg in Tennessee starting in the fourth week of June?

A. *These harassing actions made it impossible to move against Grant at Vicksburg.*

Q. Beginning on the twenty-fifth of June, Jeb Stuart began another raid around the Union army. He captured a considerable amount of supplies, but this raid proved to be a crucial mistake. Why?

A. *Stuart and his cavalry were General Lee's antennae, keeping him informed of the whereabouts of Union forces. In making this raid, Stuart went so far to the east that he became trapped beyond the Union line. Lee was thus deprived of vital information and did not have a clear idea of the positioning of the opposing army. Stuart was unable to get back to Lee until the second day of the Battle of Gettysburg.*

Q. In mid-month, General Hooker had sent a message to Lincoln saying that the Confederate force was too large for the Army of the Potomac to prevent its advance. What did this new evidence of Hooker's seeming fear of Lee cause Lincoln to do?

A. *Speed up the process of replacing Hooker with another general. He chose General George Gordon Meade, who was not well known to the rank and file, or even many of the officers, of the Army of the Potomac. However, he had a quality that Lincoln felt was imperative: Meade was not afraid of Lee or anything else. And, in fact, Lincoln had finally found the right man. Meade would remain in command of the Army of the Potomac for the remainder of the war.*

Q. Meade was not appointed until June 28. By then, were the vanguard of the Confederate forces still south of Gettysburg or farther north?

The Civil War Quiz Book

A. *Troops under General Ewell had passed as much as forty miles to the northeast of Gettysburg. One column had captured Carlisle, Pennsylvania, and was moving on the state capital at Harrisburg; another had taken York and Wrightsville.*

Q. The Confederate army was living off the Pennsylvania countryside, as Lee had planned. What was the drawback to this situation?

A. *With no supply line, the Confederate army had to keep moving as it exhausted the supplies in a given area. The Army of Northern Virginia was thus spread out over a larger area than had ever been the case before.*

Q. What did the fact that the great battle took place at Gettysburg and not elsewhere have to do with shoes?

A. *A Confederate brigade approached Gettysburg on June 30 in order to seize a supply of shoes that they had learned were in storage in the town. But Gettysburg was under the control of the Union cavalry, and the Confederates decided to return the next day with a larger force. That this decisive battle should have occurred at Gettysburg was sheer accident. One of Ewell's brigades had already passed through it on the way to York.*

Q. On the first day of the Battle of Gettysburg, fighting began with an engagement between General John Buford's Union cavalry and a division of slow advancing Confederate infantry. Buford believed that the land around Gettysburg was good terrain for a battle and determined to hold the line as long as possible. He sent a message to General John Reynolds, a few miles to the south, to bring up his infantry. By chance, that infantry included one of the toughest and most famous brigades in the Union army. What was the nickname of this brigade of men from western states?

A. *It was called the Iron Brigade and on that July 1, it more than justified its reputation, continuing to fight despite staggering losses. Two thirds of the Iron Brigade died at Gettysburg.*

Q. General Reynolds, a greatly liked and highly respected officer, was shot and killed by a Confederate sharpshooter hiding in a barn belonging to a Pennsylvania farmer named McLean (who would show up again at Appomattox). With Reynolds's death, command was temporarily given over to man whose name is a part of baseball legend. Name him.

A. *Major General Abner Doubleday, who would be credited with inventing the game of baseball. These claims are no longer considered valid.*

Q. As the day wore on, reinforcements from both armies arrived at Gettysburg. What was peculiar about the direction from which they came?

A. *Many Confederate troops came down from north of Gettysburg while many of the Union troops came up from south of it.*

Q. The Confederate reinforcements got to Gettysburg more quickly than the Union ones, and the Army of the Potomac was forced back through the town of Gettysburg to hilly ground to the south. Name the four most famous of these ridges and hills.

A. *Cemetery Hill, Cemetery Ridge, Little Round Top, and Big Round Top. If the battle was to be won, these sites had to be held.*

Q. General Doubleday was in command at Gettysburg for only a short time. General Oliver O. Howard soon arrived and took over. But as soon as General Meade heard that General Reynolds was dead he sent forward General Winfield S. Hancock to take charge. Why was General Howard unhappy about this?

A. *Doubleday, Howard, and Hancock had all been promoted to major general on the same day, November 29, 1862, but Howard was technically the senior officer. Both Howard and Hancock were remarkable men. Howard was the founder and first president of Washington, D.C.'s Howard University from 1869 to 1874 and subsequently became superintendent of West Point. Hancock was the Democratic nominee for president in 1880, but was very narrowly defeated by James Garfield.*

Q. By the late afternoon of the first day of the battle that would change the war, Union troops had retreated to but were holding the ridges and hills to the south of Gettysburg. For a hundred years afterward it was said by many, whether historian or Confederate partisan, that if *only* the forces of General Ewell had attacked again, the Army of the Potomac could have been driven from those heights where they were still trying to get organized, and the battle would have been won by the South that day. In more recent years, numerous reasons have been suggested as to why that "only" was really wishful thinking. The following answer contains five such reasons. Can you come up with three of them?

1863

A. 1. *It is important to look who was saying that the South could have won that afternoon. First and foremost, it had always been unreconstructed Confederates who refused to deal in realistic terms with why the South lost the war. As for the historians, most tried to be fair, whatever their sympathies. But some of the Southern historians looked for excuses and some of the Northern ones seemed to be intent on saying, "See, you botched it."*

  2. Even though the Union forces had suffered heavier losses, they occupied the higher ground, which is always more difficult to take.

  3. The Confederate army had also taken terrific losses the first day of the battle and its men were exhausted. There is a point beyond which men cannot fight effectively.

  4. Although Ewell was given the blame, Lee himself was there and did not order a fresh attack.

  5. Stonewall Jackson, who would probably have tried it against all odds, was dead, his body buried in one place and his amputated arm in another.

Q. Lee had decided to attack the Union forces where they stood, and ordered General Longstreet and General Ewell to strike at both flanks of the Union line simultaneously. A. P. Hill was to remain at the center, prepared to reinforce on either side or move forward himself if the situation seemed to warrant it. There was a long delay in getting ready for this attack, however—Longstreet did not get his men into position on the east, in front of Big and Little Round Tops until midafternoon. Why was Longstreet later accused by many Southerners of having lost the day by being sulky?

A. *Longstreet had suggested an entirely different plan, which involved flanking the Union army to the south and then coming in behind it. Lee overruled this idea because he*

141

simply did not know where the rest of Meade's army was, and because Jeb Stuart was still not on hand to find out for him.

Q. General Daniel Sickles in the meantime had moved his corps forward from Cemetery Ridge to what he regarded as a better position in the area known as the Peach Orchard. Did he have Meade's permission to do this?

A. *No, and it nearly led to disaster, because when Longstreet did attack, Sickles's men were in an exposed position nearly a mile out in front of the remainder of the Union line. Even with reinforcements, the Peach Orchard and adjacent Wheat Field could not be held, and the soldiers fell back into a rocky area that they named the Devil's Den.*

Q. Since Sickles had moved forward, what Union troops held Little Round Top?

A. *There was only a group from the Signal Corps there. Fortunately, this was discovered by General G. K. Warren, the chief engineer of the Army of the Potomac. He rode immediately for help, diverting troops who were moving forward toward the Peach Orchard, and then rounded up a field artillery group, who managed to get their guns up the steep, rocky incline just in time to take on Longstreet's advancing troops.*

Q. The Union army was now in trouble at the center, however, in the area between the Round Tops and Cemetery Ridge. General Hancock sent one of the best regiments in the army, the 1st Minnesota, to plug the hole. They made a famous charge and held the position. How many of the men in the regiment were killed or wounded in this engagement?

A. *Nearly 80 percent. They were entirely unsupported but showed a tenacity perhaps unequaled in the history of warfare.*

Q. All up and down the line that hot afternoon, the Confederate forces charged, and the Union line seemed on the verge of being broken several times at various points. But Meade was able to get reinforcements into the right areas at crucial moments, and as darkness set in, the Union position was essentially what it had been that morning. General Meade told his officers that he expected Lee to strike at the center the following day, having failed on both flanks. Was he correct?

A. *Yes. A division commanded by General George Pickett had finally arrived. Lee planned to have them charge the center while General Ewell's forces once again attacked Culp's Hill on the western end of the Union line, where the Confederates had come closest to success on July 2.*

Q. Why did Ewell's men begin the fighting at Culp's Hill the next day before Pickett's forces were ready to move?

A. *They had no choice, being halfway up the hill already. Unless they retreated, they would be easy targets. So they immediately tried to move forward, but had been repulsed before Pickett's charge could get under way.*

Q. For more than an hour, beginning at noon, there was a strange unnerving silence over the battlefield as the Union troops lay waiting and the Confederates moved into position under a blazing sun. Then at seven minutes past one, the Confederate artillery, nearly 150 guns, opened fire, and the Union army returned it. This artillery exchange lasted for nearly two hours. Bruce Catton has described it as "the loudest noise, probably, that had ever been heard on the North American continent up to that moment." How far away could the crashing of the guns be heard?

   a. 40 miles
   b. 70 miles
   c. 140 miles

A. *It could be heard in Pittsburgh, 140 miles away.*

Q. As the guns quieted, the nearly 15,000 Confederate soldiers, spearheaded by Pickett's division, did something that stunned the watching Union army. What was it?

A. *They came out of the woods and lined up along an entire mile of open ground in parade-ground formality. General Longstreet said afterward that he was convinced the attack would fail, and he was almost unable to give the command to begin it.*

Q. The odds against the Confederates were great. For the first time in the course of the war they were attacking the Army of the Potomac in a position chosen by the North, and on its home ground. Yet there was a moment when it seemed as though the South might carry the day in spite of everything. A force led by General Lewis Armistead, who carried his hat aloft on his sword, broke through the Union line at dead center. Only minutes later, however, Armistead had been mortally wounded, and gradually the Confederates began retreating all along the line, driven back by Union reinforcements that were rushed from point to point. Then it was over, and as Union stretcher-bearers walked among the thousands of fallen bodies that covered the battlefield, looking for those still alive, they came upon Armistead, who was able to get out a few words asking them to carry a message to an old friend. Who was this friend?

A. *Union General Winfield Scott Hancock, who had been instrumental in choosing to make a stand at Cemetery Ridge. As it happened, Hancock was being carried from the field himself, having been shot from his horse. Hancock would not be able to return to action for months, but Armistead died on the field at Gettysburg. Two years earlier, Hancock had given his close friend Armistead, and other officers who were joining the Confederate cause, a farewell party at a military base in California.*

Q. The total of killed or wounded on both sides at the Battle of Gettysburg was a staggering 40,000 men. For which side were the casualties greater?

A. *The Confederate army suffered greater losses, with about 800 more men killed, for a total of 3,903, and more than 4,000 more men wounded, for a total of 18,735. Both sides also listed more than 5,000 missing. Some of these were taken prisoner, but many of them undoubtedly had decided they had had enough of the war for the time being, and gone home.*

Q. Even as Lee was withdrawing his army on July 4, General Pemberton was surrendering Vicksburg to Grant. The people of the city were on the verge of starvation, the Union bombardment continued unabated, and there was no choice but to surrender. How long would it be before the citizens of Vicksburg, Mississippi, celebrated Independence Day again?

A. *They did not celebrate the Fourth until 1945, after the surrender of Nazi Germany.*

Q. How soon did Lincoln learn of the surrender of Vicksburg?

A. *He did not learn about it until the seventh, when a message from Admiral Porter reached Washington.*

Q. Because of the large number of Confederate soldiers captured at Vicksburg, Grant decided to "parole" them. What did this mean?

A. *They were required to sign a pledge that they would not fight again until informed that a Union prisoner had been exchanged for them.*

Q. On July 8, there was another Confederate surrender. Where did it take place?

A. *At the besieged Port Hudson. Now the entire length of the Mississippi was in Union hands.*

Q. After the Battle of Gettysburg, the Union army was very slow to pursue Lee, which disturbed Lincoln and tempered his joy at the fall of Vicksburg. Lee had moved into Maryland with the intention of crossing the Potomac back into Virginia. But the river was so swollen by storms that Lee had to wait at Williamsport, Maryland. Did Meade finally catch up to Lee?

A. *Yes, but too late. Leaving campfires burning as a subterfuge, Lee began to get his army across the river on the twelfth.*

Q. On July 11, the first names of draftees were drawn in New York City, in accordance with the Enrollment Act passed the previous March. What did this lead to two days later?

1863

A. *The beginning of the four-day draft riots in New York. Other cities had problems too, but the New York riots were by far the most severe. Draft offices, other government property, Protestant churches associated with the abolitionist movement, and the ground floor of Horace Greeley's* Tribune *were burned. Homes of some well-known Republicans were looted. The New York City police simply could not contain a situation that involved as many as 50,000 rioters.*

Q. The great majority of the rioters were Irish Catholics, and their rage was particularly directed toward blacks. Was this sheer prejudice, or was there more to it?

A. *Much of it was sheer prejudice, but blacks had recently been used as scab workers when Irish workers went on strike, setting the stage for the violence against blacks throughout the riots.*

Q. How were the riots finally put down?

A. *Troops were rushed back north from Gettysburg, ultimately 20,000 of them, and they opened fire on the mobs. Popular myth that 1,000 people were killed exaggerates the death toll by almost ten times, but it remains the worst riot in American history.*

Q. On Morris Island in Charleston Harbor, Union troops made the second attack in six days on the fortified Battery Wagner on July 18. The Union losses were enormous, with more than 1,500 casualties. What Massachusetts regiment showed particular bravery and was particularly hard hit?

A. *The Massachusetts 54th, the black regiment commanded by Colonel R. G. Shaw, who was killed.*

Q. On July 24, General Meade, still in pursuit of Lee, moved into the Shenandoah Valley through Manassas Gap. What did he find?

A. *More abandoned camps, just as had happened at Williamsport. Confederate troops had delayed the Union forces at Manassas Gap just long enough for the Confederates to get away. Now there was no chance of delivering Lee the final blow that Lincoln had hoped would win the war.*

Q. General John Hunt Morgan, the famous Confederate raider, was captured at New Lisbon, Ohio, on July 26. Who had ordered him to penetrate this far north?

A. *No one. In fact, he had disobeyed General Bragg's order not to cross the Ohio River. Since the eighth of the month, Morgan had been galloping about through Indiana and then Ohio, causing a panic in Cincinnati but meeting more and more opposition and losing more and more of his men to stiffening resistance. It had been Morgan's hope that this raid would arouse the Copperheads even further against the war, but in the end it just got him and his men confined to the Ohio Penitentiary.*

Q. What weighed two hundred pounds and was nicknamed the "Swamp Angel"?

A. *A gun that fired incendiary shells. The Union put it in place at Charleston Harbor in early August as continued action was taken against Battery Wagner and Fort Sumter. Despite heavy bombardment of the two forts, no breaches were opened that could be taken advantage of. Three weeks later, the Swamp Angel blew up while being fired and caused a number of Union casualties.*

Q. Who offered his resignation to Jefferson Davis on August 8?

A. *General Lee, who had taken all blame for the failure at Gettysburg. The offer was refused by Davis, who still felt that Lee was utterly irreplaceable.*

Q. In mid-August, President Lincoln personally tested an invention of Christopher Miner Spencer that was to give the Union cavalry, and to some extent the infantry, a new advantage in the later stages of the war. What was the invention?

A. *It was a breech-loaded seven-shot carbine rifle that was a great advance over the muzzle-loaded rifles available to the Confederates.*

Q. What were Cole, James, John, and Robert Younger, as well as Frank James, involved in at Lawrence, Kansas, on August 21, 1863?

A. *A massacre of 150 citizens of the abolitionist town in a raid led by Confederate guerrilla William Clarke Quantrill, who came to be called the "Bloodiest Man in American History." This band of outlaws, whom even many Confederates found repellent, killed every male of whatever age in the town, which they then set fire to. Robert Younger was only twelve at the time. Jesse James would join Quantrill when he was seventeen.*

Q. From mid-August on, Lincoln's main preoccupation was with Tennessee. With Lee driven back in the east and the Mississippi under Union control, the next step had to be an invasion of the industrial regions of the South, from the capital at Richmond down through the Carolinas and Georgia. Chattanooga, Tennessee, was the clear entryway into the region—that was obvious to both Northern and Southern leaders. But Lincoln also badly wanted to occupy Knoxville in eastern Tennessee. Why was this objective so important to him?

A. *The people of eastern Tennessee had been strongly pro-Union from the start, but after two years the area was still under Confederate control.*

Q. General Burnside had been training the Army of the Ohio for several months for an anticipated move into Tennessee. On September 2, he was able to take Knoxville without resistance. Why had the Confederate force at Knoxville been withdrawn?

A. *To reinforce General Bragg's army at Chattanooga.*

Q. Why, then, did General Bragg withdraw from Chattanooga?

A. *Because he knew that General Rosecrans's Army of the Cumberland was heading south, and suspected that the Union intent was to trap Bragg's Army of Tennessee in Chattanooga and lay siege to the city.*

Q. What mistaken assumption did General Rosecrans make when he found that Bragg had withdrawn from Chattanooga?

A. *He assumed that Bragg was in full retreat. In order to pursue him more quickly, he divided his army into three parts so as to take better advantage of the few mountain roads in the area. This meant that there were almost forty miles between the left and right units of his army.*

Q. Rosecrans had made a serious mistake, because Bragg was preparing to attack, and was not in fact retreating. But Bragg made a mistake of his own, assuming that there were only two Union forces. His plan was to attack the center first and then go after the left. He ordered the first attack on September 10 but it was not launched. Why?

A. *Bragg was having serious problems with his subordinates, who disliked him and distrusted him. Several of the generals under him had been trying to get him removed from command for months, but Jefferson Davis was a staunch supporter of Bragg and would not do it. Bragg was a stern man, given to fits of temper, and he had a bad habit of blaming subordinates if anything went wrong. A careful planner, he was not good at improvising and had failed several times to follow through after a victory, most notably at Murfreesboro. As a tactician, he could be brilliant in terms of setting up an attack, but by September 1863 the bad blood between himself and his generals was such that if they did not like an order they simply took it as discretionary. Not only did they refuse to attack on the tenth, but did so twice more in the next three days.*

Q. How did General Rosecrans come to realize that his army was in danger?

A. *The maneuverings of Bragg's army in preparation for the attacks that did not take place alerted him.*

Q. By the time the Battle of Chickamauga, called after the creek of that name, took place on September 19, Rosecrans had managed to pull his army together. But, to his disadvantage, General Longstreet and his divisions arrived from Virginia that very afternoon and would play a crucial role on the second day of the battle. Did either side gain any significant ground on the first day of the battle?

A. *No, although there was fierce fighting and a high casualty count.*

Q. The second day of the Battle of Chickamauga is widely regarded as the most confusing engagement in the entire war. What was the cause of the confusion?

    a. The weather
    b. The terrain
    c. The smoke

A. *All three played a part, with morning fog and a battlefield enshrouded in smoke that was kept from dissipating by the humidity of the day, but it was the terrain that was the main problem. The area was so densely wooded that even the generals involved often had no idea where their troops were. As for the soldiers themselves, they often did not know whether a force coming toward them was friend or foe and many troops on both sides were in fact killed or wounded by friendly fire.*

Q. Rosecrans kept moving divisions around in order to shore up weak points. But the chaos on the bloody field of battle caused him to make a terrible mistake. What was it?

A. *Because he did not know where his troops really were, he issued an order that moved an entire division under the command of General Thomas John Wood to the left—which left an enormous hole in the Union line. Wood had recently been reprimanded by Rosecrans for not carrying out an order quickly enough; thus on this day he jumped to obey an order that he probably should have challenged.*

Q. General Longstreet then had his men charge through the quarter-mile gap. To what extent should Longstreet's tactical abilities be lauded in this situation?

A. *Longstreet was the beneficiary of pure luck, but he did take advantage of it immediately.*

Q. As Longstreet broke through and divided the Union line in half, how did Rosecrans react?

A. *As the entire right flank of his army came apart, running for their lives, General Rosecrans and his subordinate officers quickly retreated back to Chattanooga.*

Q. General Rosecrans believed that his entire army had been routed. Was this correct?

A. *No. Although steadily pushed back on the right, General George H. Thomas gathered his troops on the top of the steep slopes at Snodgrass Hill, and kept full control over his men while entire other Union divisions were fleeing.*

Q. What was the nickname given General Thomas after his stand on Snodgrass Hill?

A. *The "Rock of Chickamauga." In an almost impregnable position, his troops turned back the majority of Bragg's army, which came at them in one wave after another. Just as they were running out of ammunition, Thomas was reinforced by General Gordon Granger, whose troops had been held in reserve to the north, and who came to the rescue without orders. Together, Thomas and Granger held the hill until dark and then retreated successfully to Chattanooga. Without Thomas, the battle would have been a complete rout. The losses on both sides were great, but oddly, considering the fact that so much of the Union army fled the scene, the casualties for the two days were higher on the Confederate side, which listed more than 2,000 dead, and nearly 15,000 wounded. There were about 500 fewer Union dead and about 5,000 fewer wounded.*

Q. Why didn't General Bragg immediately pursue the defeated Army of the Cumberland?

A. *Apparently he was unnerved by the huge losses his army had suffered. He simply ignored the urgings of General Longstreet and others to march on Chattanooga the next day. And so, like Meade on the other side after Gettysburg, he lost a "golden opportunity."*

Q. Why did the White House go into mourning on December 22 for the Confederate general Ben Hardin Helm, who had died of wounds received at Chickamauga?

A. *Helm was the husband of Mary Todd Lincoln's half sister and had been a close friend of the president.*

Q. General Bragg finally ordered an attack on Chattanooga, but discovered that the Union army had had time enough to dig in thoroughly. What did he then decide to do?

A. *Lay siege to the city, which was fairly easy to do since Chattanooga is surrounded by mountains.*

Q. General Hooker and his corps of 20,000 men were detached from Meade's Army of the Potomac on September 25 and sent by rail to Bridgeport, Alabama. Why?

A. *Bridgeport is situated just over the state line from Tennessee, only thirty miles southwest of Chattanooga. Hooker was there to assist Rosecrans, but even as he arrived in Bridge-*

port on October 2, having made the 1,200-mile journey from Virginia in an astonishingly fast trip for the time, the Confederate cavalry succeeded in closing the supply route between Bridgeport and Chattanooga.

Q. Under General Joseph Wheeler, the Confederate cavalry destroyed a bridge at Stones River on the fifth of October, severing another Union supply line. How desperate had the situation become at Chattanooga in terms of supplies?

A. *It was serious and deteriorating. Since it was impossible to feed even soldiers and horses adequately, draft mules were allowed to die by the hundreds.*

Q. Whom did Lincoln describe as being "confused and stunned like a duck hit on the head"?

A. *General Rosecrans. Something clearly had to be done. The first step was to consolidate the Armies of the Ohio, the Cumberland, and the Tennessee into a new entity called the Military Division of the Mississippi, which was placed under the command of General Grant.*

Q. Who made the decision to replace General Rosecrans with General Thomas, the hero of Chickamauga?

A. *Grant was given a choice between the two men by Secretary of War Stanton and chose Thomas. The changeover had been made by the time Grant arrived in Chattanooga on October 24.*

Q. Grant's first move at Chattanooga was to open what the Union soldiers immediately dubbed "the cracker line." What was it?

The Civil War Quiz Book

A. *A new supply line, established by building a pontoon bridge at Brown's Ferry on the Tennessee River in an area only lightly defended by the Confederates. Not only was the supply problem solved, but General Hooker's troops were able to join those at Chattanooga.*

Q. While the Union position at Chattanooga was being strengthened, General Bragg was weakening his own. There was so much dissension among his subordinates that several of them had actually called for Bragg's replacement while Bragg was in the room during a visit to the command post by Jefferson Davis. General Longstreet, who was one of Bragg's greatest critics, was not willing to take command himself since he regarded himself as an essential unit of Lee's Army of Northern Virginia. Davis did not like any of the other suggestions made to him since they involved generals he did not have confidence in. He did transfer General Leonidas ''Bishop'' Polk to a new command in Mississippi. He also made a suggestion concerning Longstreet which Bragg finally acted on in the first week of November. What did Bragg order Longstreet to do?

A. *He sent him to reinforce the small Confederate force that was harassing General Burnside at Knoxville. He thus reduced his own forces by 20,000.*

Q. In Virginia, in what is known as the Bristoe Campaign, the forces of Meade and Lee had been involved in numerous skirmishes and small battles since early October. What was the chief result of these engagements?

A. *Several thousand casualties, heaviest on the Confederate side, with no real gain by either army.*

Q. What general, a personal favorite of Grant's, arrived in the Chattanooga area with 17,000 men on November 15?

A. *General Sherman.*

Q. Who was Edward Everett and where did he give a two-hour speech on November 19?

A. *Edward Everett, a former representative, senator, and governor of Massachusetts, gave the main speech at the dedication of the military cemetery at Gettysburg. Lincoln's ten-sentence speech followed and was politely received but it would be some time before it was fully recognized as the great address it is.*

Q. Despite the buildup of Union forces at Chattanooga, what did the confident Braxton Bragg regard the Union troops as?

A. *His "prisoners."*

Q. The battle of Chattanooga was played out over the course of three days. The action on November 23 was in a sense merely a prelude but it was carried out in a spectacular manner. The 25,000 troops under General Thomas appeared outside the city, on the flat ground beneath the heights of Missionary Ridge, which ran from due east of the city around toward the south. The Confederates on the ridge watched as the Union soldiers marched back and forth in what was obviously a drill or parade display. The Confederates were quite enjoying the spectacle when suddenly things changed. What happened?

A. *The entire Union force suddenly wheeled and charged Orchard Knob, a knoll that lay between Missionary Ridge and the city and was the Confederate position closest to the city. The small Confederate force there didn't have a chance.*

The Bettmann Archive

Q. This engraving shows the attack on what at Chattanooga?

A. *Lookout Mountain. This engraving shows one of the reasons why the Confederates believed that their position on Lookout Mountain could not possibly be taken. Crags and sheer drops can be found all over the site. The actual November 24 battle was fought some five hundred feet below the summit. Hooker's men initially came up the west side, and then turned north. There was a lot of fog that day, which is why the battle has come to be known by the picturesque nickname "The Battle Above the Clouds." The fighting was difficult, but the Union troops outnumbered the Confederates almost six to one, and although the Confederates fought bravely, retreating slowly around Lookout Mountain to the north, there was no choice but to withdraw the troops to the main Confederate stronghold on Missionary Ridge during the night.*

Q. While Hooker was taking Lookout Mountain, General Sherman assaulted what his maps indicated was the northern end of Missionary Ridge. He took it but was greeted by an unpleasant surprise. What was it?

A. *The maps had been wrong. What he had captured was an outlying hill that was completely separated from the main ridge by a ravine that was seriously vulnerable to enemy fire.*

Q. The plan that Grant had drawn up for the following day called for Sherman to attack along the northern end of Missionary Ridge while Hooker was to march forward from Lookout Mountain on the southern end of the ridge. But Hooker had trouble advancing because of trees felled across the road and a crucial bridge that had been destroyed by the retreating Lookout Mountain troops the previous night. Sherman had to go up against an oversize division led by General Patrick Cleburne, a tenacious Irish-born fighter whose troops were the toughest in all of Bragg's army. Even though Sherman had larger numbers, attack after attack across the ravine on Cleburne's entrenched troops failed. Sherman in fact was faced with a vastly more difficult task than Hooker had dealt with in his much-romanticized victory at Lookout Mountain. Grant changed his plan and ordered General Thomas's corps to mount an attack on the center at Missionary Ridge that was originally supposed to take place only after Sherman and Hooker had made progress. Thomas's men were supposed to take the forward rifle pits and then pause to regroup. What soon caused Grant to turn angrily on Thomas, who remained with him at Orchard Knob?

A. *After taking the rifle pits, Thomas's troops, instead of halting as ordered, kept going up Missionary Ridge. Grant thought Thomas had changed the orders and not told him, but in fact the troops had made the decision for themselves. They were in a much more exposed position than Grant had recognized would be the case, and so they went charging forward up the steep slope.*

Q. In an hour, the oncoming Union divisions had driven the Confederates from Missionary Ridge, except for Cleburne's division at the northern end. The Confederates broke and ran all along the line. Which of the following *cannot* be considered a valid explanation of the Confederate collapse?

    a. The soldiers on the ridge had a clear view of the size of the Union army and could see that they were heavily outnumbered.

    b. Many of these troops were fairly green and unused to combat.

    c. The constant infighting among Bragg's officers had percolated down to demoralize the infantry.

A. *The invalid reason is b. These were highly seasoned troops. They had never broken like this before, and it would never happen again, but a combination of the other two factors clearly caused them to lose their nerve on November 25, 1863.*

Q. The next day the Union army went in pursuit of the defeated Confederates retreating toward Atlanta. Who held them off long enough for the main army to escape?

A. *Pat Cleburne was at it again, the only Confederate officer at the Battle of Chattanooga who could be said to have played a hero's role.*

Q. In very cold weather, General Longstreet launched an attack on Knoxville, which he had been besieging to little effect. The attack was also ineffective, and with reinforcements approaching from the victorious Union army at Chattanooga, Longstreet withdrew to winter quarters. Swelled with the success of his victory by default, what did General Burnside fail to do?

A. *As was his custom, he did not pursue Longstreet, which meant that Grant had to keep a considerable force in the area for months.*

Q. General Braxton Bragg's resignation was accepted on November 30 by Jefferson Davis. He took more than two weeks to appoint a new permanent head of the Army of Tennessee. What was the reason for the delay?

A. *It was obvious that he must appoint General Joseph Johnston to the post but he had been feuding with Johnston over matters large and small since shortly after First Bull Run, and he was furious with Johnston for not having tried to attack Grant's rear at Vicksburg—although that would have been practically suicidal considering how few men he had under his command at the time. Davis finally bowed to the inevitable, but the strained relationship between the two men would cause further problems down the line.*

Q. Encouraged by the victory at Chattanooga, Lincoln decided that the time was right to begin to look further into the future. What Proclamation did he issue on December 8?

A. *The Proclamation of Amnesty and Reconstruction was used to close his annual message to Congress. Lincoln offered pardons and amnesty to all those who took an oath of allegiance to the United States, and accepted its laws, including those concerning slavery. Confederate government officials and high-ranking members of the military (as well as members of the U.S. military who had gone over to the Confederate side) were not included in the amnesty.*

Q. With the armies in winter quarters, December was a quiet month on the military fronts. Where, however, did a bombardment that had been going on since August continue on an almost daily basis?

A. *At Charleston Harbor's Fort Sumter. The fort had been reduced virtually to rubble, but it was rubble that could not be taken so long as it was manned. The refusal to capitulate at Fort Sumter prefigured the stubbornness of the Confederates in the year to come.*

Part Five
1864

Q. In the last months of 1863, soldiers on both sides—but particularly Confederate soldiers—increasingly took to challenging farm animals like hogs and cattle and demanding that they give a password. Why?

A. *Because when no password was forthcoming, the livestock was shot and eaten. If objections were raised, the soldiers would say that, getting no response, they had assumed they were dealing with an enemy sympathizer. Food was in such short supply in the South during the winter of 1864 that in early January Jefferson Davis gave General Lee authority to commandeer food supplies in Virginia from its own citizens.*

Q. Name the Confederate hero who turned up in Richmond at the end of the first week of January after escaping from a Northern prison.

A. *John Hunt Morgan could not be held by the walls of the Ohio Penitentiary.*

Q. In what border state did pro-Union leaders propose that a convention should be set up to write a new constitution that outlawed slavery?

A. *Tennessee. Lincoln's Proclamation of Amnesty and Reconstruction was beginning to have the effect he had hoped for.*

Q. On February 1, Congress restored the rank of lieutenant general in the United States Army. Who was the last person who had held this rank?

A. *George Washington. By restoring this rank, Congress made it possible for Lincoln to move toward appointing General Grant as overall commander of Union forces without ruffling quite as many military feathers. Whoever was given this rank would automatically outrank anyone else.*

Q. Leaving Vicksburg in early February with 25,000 men, General Sherman headed toward Meridian, Mississippi. With the smaller, and more scattered, army of General Leonidas Polk steadily falling back from Sherman's advance, the Union general occupied Meridian by February 14. What was the military significance of this small city?

A. *It was the most important railroad center in central Mississippi. Sherman's troops spent almost a week in and around Meridian, tearing up the railroad lines and destroying its warehouses, arsenals, even its hospitals and hotels. If the South had been able to see this as the portent of things to come that it was, its people would certainly have experienced a collective shiver of dread.*

Q. At the end of February, a prison for captured Union soldiers began operating at a small town near Americus, Georgia. The prison was originally called Camp Sumter, but soon came to be known by another name. What was that name?

A. *Andersonville, which was the name of the town where it was located; it soon became the most infamous of all Confederate prisoner-of-war camps.*

Q. Two weeks earlier, slightly over half of the 109 Union officers who had escaped from Libby Prison in Richmond were successful in reaching the safety of Union lines. Their reports of the conditions at Libby spurred a raid on Richmond by a 3,500-man cavalry unit under General Judson Kilpatrick. He was to be joined by another 500 men commanded by Colonel Ulric Dahlgren, who had lost a leg at Gettysburg. Both forces ran into unexpected problems around the lightly defended Confederate capital, and retreated. On March 2, in retreat, Dahlgren was killed. Papers found on his body suggested that it was his and Kilpatrick's intention not only to free Union prisoners but also to burn the city and carry out an additional act whose mere suggestion caused outrage in the South. What was this supposed additional "objective"?

A. *The killing of Jefferson Davis and his Cabinet. Copies of these papers were sent by Lee to General Meade, who denied knowing anything about them. This matter remains unsettled to this day, with some suggesting that Meade was lying and others saying that the papers were forged by Confederates.*

Q. General Grant was officially commissioned as lieutenant general at a Washington ceremony attended by Lincoln and his Cabinet on March 9. Now General-in-Chief, did Grant make large-scale changes in command of the various Union armies?

A. *No, but the ones he did make were significant. Since he wanted to be in the field, not in Washington, he kept General Halleck on as Chief of Staff. To his own command in the west he appointed General Sherman. And to bolster the cavalry of the Army of the Potomac, he brought General Philip Sheridan east to join Meade, who remained as overall commander of the Army of the Potomac, with which Grant made his own field headquarters.*

The Civil War Quiz Book

Q. The day after Grant was given command over all the Union forces, a campaign began under General Nathaniel Banks to take control of the remainder of Louisiana. Had this endeavor, which came to be called the Red River Campaign, been Grant's idea?

A. *No. He had in fact opposed it, believing that Union control of the Mississippi rendered the campaign irrelevant. He wanted his troops concentrated east of the Mississippi. But preparations for the Red River Campaign, which had been planned by General Halleck, were too far along to halt it.*

Q. General Banks was still derided in the South with the nickname "Commissary" because of the supplies he had left behind after being routed by Stonewall Jackson in the Shenandoah Valley. Did the Red River Campaign revive his reputation?

A. *Quite the opposite. The Red River Campaign, which lasted nearly two months, was a mess almost from start to finish. Banks's troops did capture a fair amount of cotton, but they also did a lot of general pillaging, which was hardly the way to go about winning the hearts and minds of a state Lincoln hoped to win back to the Union with his Reconstruction policies. What's more, despite a few military successes, Banks was eventually outmaneuvered by General Richard Taylor, who was the son of President Zachary Taylor and the brother-in-law of Jefferson Davis.*

Q. What did a convention in Arkansas ratify in mid-March?

A. *A new constitution that abolished slavery. The border states were beginning to throw in their lot with a future that would see an end to slavery.*

1864

Q. Grant was in Nashville conferring with General Sherman on March 17 and back in Washington meeting with President Lincoln on the twenty-fourth. Was Grant planning to move against General Johnston's forces in Georgia, General Lee's army in Virginia, or both?

A. *He was planning a move against both. Sherman was to attack Johnston at Dalton, Georgia, and drive toward Atlanta. Meade was to attack Lee in Virginia and move toward Richmond. Grant himself would accompany Meade. In addition, General Banks was supposed to turn around and move on Mobile, Alabama, by April 15. General Benjamin Butler (Beast Butler to Confederates because of his New Orleans Woman Order) was to cut the rail lines between Richmond and Petersburg, Virginia. General Franz Sigel was to control the Shenandoah Valley. This was the first grand strategic design of the war on either side, one that made use of multiple armies playing a specific role in an ensemble action. Unfortunately, some of the actors weren't up to those roles.*

Q. Generals Butler, Banks, and Sigel were all ''political generals.'' What did this mean?

A. *They were appointed not because of their military experience (neither Butler nor Banks had any) but because their appointments succeeded in bolstering the support of various political or ethnic groups for the war. Butler had been a very successful criminal lawyer in Massachusetts, but more important, he was a prominent Peace Democrat. When he supported Lincoln on the war, his conversion to War Democrat made him an important political symbol. Banks was governor of Massachusetts when the war broke out, and his appointment consolidated support for the war in that state. Sigel, of German birth, had played an important part in the ill-fated revolution of 1847–48 against Austrian Emperor*

The Civil War Quiz Book

Ferdinand I. Because of his military background, he seemed a good choice to help rally German immigrant support. Sigel had been originally commissioned as a colonel, Butler as a brigadier general, and Banks as a major general. All three had spotty records, but because of their political significance, Grant knew he could not remove them. All were major generals in March of 1864.

Q. In the first week of April, General Longstreet received new orders, which greatly pleased him. What were they?

A. *At long last, he was ordered to leave Tennessee and rejoin Lee's Army of Northern Virginia.*

Q. On April 12, Nathan Bedford Forrest made a raid on the Union-held Fort Pillow in Tennessee. What happened here that would enrage the North and remain a source of controversy well into the mid-twentieth century?

A. *According to the Northern accounts, Forrest's men opened fire on the Union troops after they had surrendered, killing 231, and wounding 100. Half the Union soldiers at the fort were black troops, and these were particularly hard hit. Northern papers carried huge headlines about the "Fort Pillow Massacre." The South maintained that the Union troops had not surrendered but had tried to fight their way out. Most historians now accept that there was a massacre, but in the South the accusation is still a sore point for many.*

Q. In mid-April, Grant called a halt to all prisoner exchanges with the Confederacy until the numbers exchanged were made equal (which had not previously been the case) and black prisoners were exchanged as readily as white. The Confederacy adamantly refused to treat black prisoners as though they were white, but the break-off of prisoner exchange caused them a serious problem. What was it?

A. *Since many exchanged prisoners eventually went back into the field, still another manpower source for the dwindling Confederate army was cut off.*

Q. What phrase was added to federal coins, as required by an act of Congress, in April 1864?

A. *"In God We Trust."*

Q. Having given up the Red River Campaign, General Banks retreated to his starting point at Alexandria, Louisiana. But here he was faced with a desperate situation concerning the naval vessels that had accompanied him. What was the problem?

A. *Many of the ships were stranded because the level of the river had sunk so low. A plan was devised to raise the level of the river by building dams. The plan worked, but the last of the ships did not get out until the middle of May. Thus one aspect of Grant's plan, having Banks march into Alabama, could not be carried out.*

Q. What happened to Jefferson Davis's five-year-old son, Joseph, on April 30?

A. *In the presence of his nanny, the boy fell off the gallery railing of the Confederate White House onto the brick terrace below. He died within minutes. Thus the Confederate president was distracted with grief just as Grant began to make his move.*

Q. On May 4, General Meade's Army of the Potomac, with General Grant also present, crossed the Rapidan River and began to make its way through the heavily wooded area west of Chancellorsville, Virginia, known as the Wilderness. Was this course of action Grant's or Meade's idea?

A. *Although Meade was nominally in command, the plan was Grant's. If the Union army could get across the Wilderness quickly, it could be in a position to cut Lee off from Richmond, fifty-five miles to the south.*

Q. Lee anticipated Grant's march through the Wilderness and ordered his forces forward to meet them. He did not want to fight in the Wilderness any more than Grant did—it was a terrible place to have a battle—but he felt that was the only way to stop Grant from advancing on Richmond. To fight in the Wilderness also would diminish the impact of the larger Union force, which numbered 115,000 to Lee's 64,000. The horrors of the actual battle were greater than either Lee or Grant expected because of something that happened to the woods themselves that May 5. What was it?

A. *In many places the woods caught fire, adding to the confusion of a battle in which neither side knew at any given moment whether the troops to the left or right of them were friend or foe. An ordinarily minor leg wound, even a sprained ankle, could mean that a soldier would be burned alive, unable to flee the flames.*

Q. On the first day of the Battle of the Wilderness, the fighting was continuous from seven in the morning until eight at night. The casualties were horrendous but no decisive gain was made by the troops on either side. On May 6, the Union forces appeared to be on the verge of a breakthrough when reinforcements under General Longstreet arrived on the scene. His troops succeeded in pushing part of the Union line back, but then, in an eerie reenactment of events that had taken place a year and two days earlier, only three miles away, tragedy struck the Confederates. What happened?

A. *In the confusion of the battle, General Longstreet and General Micah Jenkins, riding together, were both shot at the same moment by their own troops, just as Stonewall Jackson had been at Chancellorsville. Longstreet was incapacitated for five months and Jenkins died of a bullet in the brain. As word of what had happened spread, the Confederate troops lost their edge.*

Q. The Battle of the Wilderness had been a draw, with 17,000 Union casualties and 7,500 Confederate. After such a draw, and with such losses, the Army of the Potomac had always withdrawn in the past. The Union troops fully expected another "skedaddle," as they called it. What did Grant order?

A. *He ordered an advance southward toward the small but crucial crossroads town of Spotsylvania, twelve miles away. Despite their exhaustion, the Union soldiers were elated. Perhaps at long last they had a commander worthy of their own extraordinary courage.*

Q. Even as the Battle of the Wilderness was drawing to an inconclusive close, on May 7, General Sherman made the first advance toward Atlanta. How many troops did he have under his command?

    a. 85,000
    b. 100,000
    c. 110,000

A. *He had 100,000 troops from three armies, that of the Cumberland, the Tennessee, and the Ohio, under Generals George Thomas, James McPherson, and John Schofield.*

Q. Grant's forces arrived at Spotsylvania on May 8, only to find Lee already there. Lee's forces were already partially dug in. What did Grant do?

A. *He ordered the Union army to dig in also, and sent a message to Washington that he intended "to fight it out on this line if it takes all summer."*

Q. On May 9, General John Sedgwick of the Army of the Potomac sat astride his horse surveying the Confederate battlements. He eyed them contemptuously and said, "They couldn't hit an elephant at this distance." What happened next?

A. *These are among the most ironic "famous last words" in history. Sedgwick was killed by a shot to the head from a Confederate bullet only seconds later. But his end was not unfitting—he had proved himself one of the most valiant of Union generals again and again, if not always the most prudent.*

Q. As the two armies dug in at Spotsylvania, General Sheridan and his cavalry had left the scene to go after what Confederate force?

A. *Sheridan had persuaded Grant to let him pursue Jeb Stuart. In the process, he was to try to disrupt the supply line for Lee's army and, if successful against Stuart, he would then move on to Richmond, which General Butler was supposed to approach from the south.*

Q. Jeb Stuart and his cavalry made a stand on May 11 at Yellow Tavern, Virginia, against Sheridan and his cavalry. What made this engagement a disaster for the Confederacy?

A. *Stuart was badly wounded and died the next day in Richmond at the age of thirty-one. His loss was a terrible blow to Lee, who had depended on the flamboyant Stuart more than anyone except Stonewall Jackson. Now they were both gone.*

Q. At Spotsylvania, the Confederate forces had built breastworks to the north of the courthouse. This defensive position was given the name the "Mule Shoe," because of its shape. What had its nickname changed to by the end of the day on May 12?

A. *The "Bloody Angle." In one of the fiercest charges of the entire war, brigade after brigade of the Union army poured over the front Confederate breastworks. The Union forces captured more than 2,000 Confederate troops, including General Edward Johnson, and took twenty cannon that the Confederates had brought forward that very morning. When the Union forces tried to advance on the second Confederate line, however, they were driven back in fighting that inflicted a dreadful toll on both sides in a battle that lasted from 4:00 A.M. until midnight.*

Q. At Spotsylvania, General Lee came forward to take personal command of troops trying to hold the second line. He had also done this at the Battle of the Wilderness. What did the troops do on both occasions?

A. *Shouted "General Lee to the rear," and refused to fight until their beloved commander was safely behind the lines.*

Q. By the conclusion of the fighting at the Bloody Angle, how many Union troops had been lost in the previous week?

   a. 19,500
   b. 24,000
   c. 30,000

A. *At least 30,000 were killed, wounded, or missing. As word of these casualties got out, people began to call Grant a "butcher" in both the North and the South. But unlike his predecessors, Grant was not afraid of such criticism. He was determined to win the war as quickly as possible, no matter what it took.*

Q. General Sherman and his three armies were flanking General Johnston in Georgia, at Dalton. Did Johnston decide to make a stand or retreat?

A. *He retreated to a new line at Resaca. Johnston, with 45,000 fewer men, was convinced that it would be disastrous to make a stand until Sherman made a mistake.*

Q. Advancing southward through the Shenandoah Valley, according to Grant's grand design, General Sigel's 6,500 men were met by Confederate cavalry on May 15. Reinforcements under General Breckinridge then succeeded in pushing Sigel back. Which side had the numerical advantage in this battle at New Market, Virginia?

A. *At 5,000 men, the Confederates were outnumbered but prevailed anyway. First Banks and now Sigel had failed to do his job—the "political" generals were erasing the detail of Grant's design.*

1864

Q. The third "political" general, Benjamin Butler, attacked Confederate forces under General Beauregard at Drewry's Bluff, Virginia, the next day, May 16. How did he fare?

A. *Miserably. In a situation that was inconclusive and still held out the possibility of victory, Butler instead withdrew to his original staging area at Bermuda Hundred. Here he was between the James and Appomattox rivers in a kind of "bottle," which was then "strongly corked," as Grant was to put it, by General Beauregard. Sheridan, who had managed to join Butler just before the Battle of Drewry's Bluff, decided to take the risk of trying to return to Grant's side, which would take him almost a week.*

Q. Deciding against further action at Spotsylvania after an aborted attack on May 18, Grant moved his and Meade's Army of the Potomac toward Hanover Junction, Virginia, but Lee again guessed what Grant was up to and got his army into position there before Grant arrived. By adroit maneuvering, Lee managed to split the Union army in two on May 23. Why did he fail to take advantage of this situation?

A. *Lee, who had been less than well for some time, was suffering from a very high fever that brought on delirium.*

Q. Throughout May General Johnston had repeatedly fallen back as Sherman mounted flanking movements. There had been several skirmishes and minor battles that took their toll on both sides, each losing about 9,000 men. How many miles closer to Atlanta, however, was Sherman by the end of May than he had been at the beginning of the month?

    a. 40 miles
    b. 60 miles
    c. 80 miles

A. *The answer is b. The Confederates were holding in the New Hope–Dallas area, only twenty-five miles northwest of Atlanta.*

Q. Grant was getting frustrated by the beginning of June. Every time he tried to move the Army of the Potomac around Lee, the Confederates managed to get ahead of him and set up new entrenchments. It had happened at North Anna River and at Totopotomoy Creek. The same was true at Cold Harbor, only a few miles northeast of Richmond, where Grant arrived on June 1. Grant decided to make an all-out attack on the entrenched Confederates. On the evening before the battle, June 2, what were many Union soldiers observed pinning to their coats?

A. *Slips of paper with their names on them, so that they could be more easily identified if they were killed.*

Q. Grant ordered an attack on the entrenched Confederates at Cold Harbor to begin at dawn on June 3. By the time he called it off at noon, at least 7,000 Union soldiers had been killed or wounded. What were Grant's feelings about this failed attack?

A. *He always regretted having ordered it. But he had learned his lesson: Even forces of lesser number that were so thoroughly dug in could not be dislodged by frontal attacks.*

Q. On June 4, the troublesome General John Frémont, who had not in fact held command since 1862, resigned from the army. What political office had he been nominated for on May 31?

A. *He had been nominated for president by a group of radical Republicans who gave ample evidence of the confusing crosscurrents among their small number by calling themselves the Radical Democratic party.*

Q. General Sigel had quickly been replaced as commander of the defeated Shenandoah Valley forces by David Hunter, who had previously caused outrage when he had declared the slaves free in the Department of the South. On June 5, he won a decisive battle at Piedmont and proceeded to occupy Staunton, Virginia. What did he do then that added to his standing as one of the most hated Union generals in the South?

A. *He carried out a policy of massive burning in the area, including the torching of the famous Virginia Military Institute.*

Q. On June 8, Lincoln was easily renominated at the Republican Convention in Baltimore. Andrew Johnson was then nominated to replace the incumbent vice-president, Hannibal Hamlin of Maine. Hamlin had been the first person to whom Lincoln had shown the Emancipation Proclamation, and the two men got along quite well. Lincoln said, however, that he would leave the selection of the vice-presidential nominee up to the convention and Hamlin did not blame Lincoln for his ouster, since he did not believe Lincoln had had anything to do with it. Was he right or wrong?

A. *Lincoln covered his tracks on this matter so well that it is still not known what he did, but there is evidence that he wanted Andrew Johnson, who as a War Democrat and military governor of Tennessee offered much better symbolic credentials. In 1889, two years before his death at the age of eighty-two, Hamlin himself decided that he had been taken in by Lincoln.*

Q. Why had General Sherman dispatched General Samuel D. Sturgis all the way back to Mississippi in early June to confront Nathan Bedford Forrest?

A. *Sherman's supply line along the railroads was now almost four hundred miles long, and Forrest was seriously threatening it. At the battle of Brice's Cross Roads, however, Forrest completely routed Sturgis, who had twice as many men as Forrest's 3,500.*

Q. While Forrest was causing problems for Sherman, Lee found it necessary to send his nephew General Fitzhugh Lee to try to stop similar raids by General Sheridan's cavalry in Virginia. Why was Sheridan delighted with this move?

A. *Because his real objective was to distract Lee from Grant's movement of his entire army south of Richmond to Petersburg, Virginia. Sheridan, however, came out on the losing side against Generals Fitzhugh Lee and Wade Hampton at Trevilian Station, and decided to rejoin Grant, although the plan had called for him to join Hunter in the Shenandoah Valley.*

Q. On June 14, the Army of the Potomac constructed a bridge across the James River, over which its forces would cross on their way to Petersburg. Why was the bridge a landmark in military history?

A. *With a span of 2,100 feet it was the longest pontoon bridge ever constructed and is not believed ever to have been surpassed.*

Q. Grant had begun to move the Army of the Potomac south on June 13, leaving behind the corps under the command of

General Warren (who had saved Little Round Top at Gettysburg) to mislead Lee. How long did it take for Lee to figure out what was happening?

A. *Four days. Lee for once had failed to anticipate Grant's move, expecting him to attack Richmond instead of the "back door" to the capital, Petersburg. Unfortunately for the Union forces, General William Farrar Smith totally threw away an opportunity to take Petersburg on the night of June 15 when he decided to wait for the arrival of the main force from Cold Harbor before attacking. But by the time the main force was present on June 18, Lee had caught on and was rapidly sending in reinforcements. An opportunity that might well have ended the war within a week had been lost, and Grant settled in for a siege that would last for nearly ten months.*

Q. On June 19, 1864, a fierce naval battle took place just off Cherbourg, France, between the Union ship, U.S.S. *Kearsarge,* under the command of Captain John A. Winslow, and the almost legendary *Alabama* under the command of Captain Raphael Semmes. Semmes had sailed the *Alabama* virtually around the world during the previous two years, capturing or sinking sixty-nine commercial ships carrying supplies for the Union. He had put into the port of Cherbourg for repairs, but when the *Kearsarge* blockaded the harbor, he decided to fight his way out. The *Alabama* was sunk after an hour's fighting, but Semmes was rescued by an English yacht. Name the great French painter who watched the battle from the cliffs at Cherbourg and painted the very uncharacteristic picture illustrated on page 184 from sketches he made at the scene.

A. *Édouard Manet, better known for his nudes. The painting now hangs in the Philadelphia Museum of Art.*

Philadelphia Museum of Art: The John G. Johnson Collection

Q. In Georgia, Sherman continued to press Johnston back toward Atlanta by outflanking him. But on June 27, Sherman got impatient and tried to attack the new Confederate entrenchments at Kennesaw Mountain, two miles northwest of Marietta, only ten miles from Atlanta at the time, and now on the city's doorstep. How many times the number of Confederate casualties did Union forces suffer in this attack?

A. *The Confederates had fewer than 300 casualties, the Union army at least seven times that number. Now Sherman too had learned Grant's hard lesson about frontal attacks.*

Q. Lee had dispatched General Jubal A. Early back into the Shenandoah Valley. After driving a small force under Franz Sigel all the way to Harpers Ferry, what did Early astonish Union generals by doing?

A. *Pushing on into Maryland toward Washington, causing panicky reactions in the capital. Reinforcements were sent to Washington on July 6.*

Q. Against what Confederate general was an outcry beginning to arise in the South?

A. *General Johnston, who on May 8, again being flanked by Sherman, moved back south of the Chattahoochee River, virtually on the outskirts of Atlanta.*

Q. To whom did Captain Oliver Wendell Holmes, Jr., the future Supreme Court justice, say, "Get down, you damn fool, or you'll be killed," on July 11 as General Early attacked Fort Stevens outside Washington?

A. *President Lincoln, who was trying to watch the battle from the parapets. A man standing next to Lincoln had just been shot dead by a sniper. Holmes himself was wounded three times in the course of the war, and had been left for dead on the battlefield at Antietam with a gunshot wound through the neck.*

Q. Early's troops retreated southward on July 13 because Union reinforcements were being put into place. Why did many on both sides think at the time that Early could actually have taken Washington, at least temporarily?

A. *Because so many of the Union reinforcements were new recruits who had never been in battle.*

Q. On July 17, General Johnston received a telegram from Jefferson Davis. What did it announce?

A. *That he was being relieved of command, to be replaced by General Hood, who was present.*

Q. Were Johnston's officers and men pleased that he had been removed?

A. *Far from it. They regarded Johnston as a real leader and brilliant tactician. For all of Hood's courage (he had had an arm amputated after Gettysburg and a leg after the Battle of Chickamauga), they did not believe he was capable of commanding an entire army. General Sherman fully agreed with this estimation of both men and was delighted at the change. The top level of the Confederate forces at Atlanta were now very much changed, since General Leonidas Polk had recently been killed by a Union artillery shell.*

Q. On July 20, General Hood put into effect a plan that had, ironically, been drawn up by General Johnston. The plan called for the Union forces to be attacked as they crossed Peachtree Creek. What went wrong?

A. *General Thomas's Army of the Cumberland had already gotten across the creek on improvised bridges before the*

Confederate attack. Although the Confederate force under General Hardee was almost as large as Thomas's 20,000-man army, Thomas held on as fiercely as he had at Chickamauga, and the Confederates retreated with a loss of nearly a quarter of their men, suffering two and half times as many casualties as the Army of the Cumberland, thanks to Thomas's effective use of cannon.

Q. A second attack was launched by Hood on July 22 against McPherson's Army of the Tennessee. Because of bad timing in launching two separate corps, the Confederates were once again driven back. But the Union suffered an important loss. What was it?

A. *General McPherson, held in extremely high regard by both Sherman and Grant, accidentally rode into a Confederate regiment, which signaled for him to surrender. Instead, he tipped his hat and rode off at full speed, but was shot from his horse and killed instantly.*

Q. On July 30, an enormous explosion took place at Petersburg. A tunnel five hundred feet long had been dug through the rock from Union positions outside the walls of Petersburg to a point that lay under the interior of the stronghold. Here explosives were set off that blew an entire Confederate regiment into the air. The resulting crater was more than 10,000 square feet in size. The plan had been for a division of black soldiers, who had been specially trained during the month it took to build the tunnel, to lead a Union charge through the tunnel, out of the crater, and into Petersburg itself. Why was the plan changed and a white division sent in instead?

A. *There has been speculation that General Meade lacked confidence in the black soldiers, despite their special training, while Grant was apparently worried that if the charge failed, he would be accused of using blacks as cannon fodder. But the change in plan proved a disaster. The commanding officer of the white division chosen to go in stayed behind getting drunk, and the Confederates were able to shoot down into the crater from above with impunity. The whites retreated, the black troops were sent in at last and were cut down in great numbers. An innovative idea turned into a disaster in its execution.*

Q. Lashed to the rigging of his flagship, the *Hartford,* Admiral David Farragut watched as the Union ironclad *Tecumseh* went down after striking a mine (then called a torpedo) and supposedly yelled out the famous words, "Damn the torpedoes, full steam ahead!" At what Southern port did this action take place on August 5?

A. *Mobile, Alabama, where Farragut and his fleet went on to carry the day, taking over the most important remaining port of call for Confederate blockade runners and setting the stage for a land attack on Mobile.*

Q. General Joseph Wheeler and the majority of the Confederate cavalry began in mid-August to harass the rail lines supplying Sherman. Why was this excursion ordered by General Hood a double-barreled mistake?

A. *Sherman's supplies were more than ample for the time being and it left Hood virtually without cavalry forces around Atlanta itself.*

Q. The photograph on page 189 shows Union soldiers destroying Confederate railroad tracks at Atlanta. What was the nickname given to the rails after the ties below them were set afire?

The Bettmann Archive

A. They were called "Sherman's neckties," since the fire caused them to bend in the middle. For good measure, they were often then bent around tree trunks.

Q. At the Democratic Convention in Chicago, what trouble-making former congressman gave the keynote address calling for an end to the war since it had failed to restore the Union?

A. *Clement Vallandigham was back in full Copperhead cry.*

Q. Even as George McClellan was being named in Chicago as the Democratic nominee for president, along with the even more antiwar congressman George Pendleton of Ohio for vice-president, what were Sherman's forces finally succeeding in doing around Atlanta?

A. *Cutting the last two rail lines into Atlanta, the Montgomery and Atlanta Line on August 30, and the even more important Macon and Weston Line on the thirty-first. General Hood began to pull out of Atlanta the following day, burning supplies that could not be carried with the Confederate troops. The first Union troops marched into Atlanta on September 2. At the beginning of August, Abraham Lincoln had resigned himself to the probable election of his former general, George McClellan, as president in November. But between the capture of Mobile Bay and the fall of Atlanta, everything had changed.*

Q. General McClellan was in a considerable pickle. He was essentially a War Democrat but was running on a platform that had largely been drawn up by extreme Peace Democrats like Vallandigham. What did he do about it?

A. *In a letter released September 8, he repudiated the plank written by Vallandigham that spoke of "four years of failure." His rationale for this was that he couldn't say such a thing to the men who fought with him, but the real problem was that the situation had changed so quickly. The Peace Democrats were enraged, and even looked for a tenable substitute candidate; in the end, platform and candidate*

188

were so at odds with one another that the Democrats were
open to ridicule. McClellan was for continuing the war (but
not to abolish slavery) while much of his party was against
the war, period.

Q. The first verse of McClellan's campaign song went like this:
"Little Mac, Little Mac, you're the very man. Go down to
Washington as soon as you can. Lincoln's got to get away
and make room for you. We must beat Lincoln and Johnson
too." What famous American songwriter composed this
below-standard work?

A. *Stephen Collins Foster, but changes in the lyrics had to be*
made, since Foster died in January 1864, and could hardly
have guessed that far in advance that Andrew Johnson would
be Lincoln's running mate.

Q. What elusive Confederate raider was surrounded and killed
in Tennessee in early September?

A. *John Hunt Morgan, who tried to flee rather than surrender*
as he had in Ohio a year earlier.

Q. General Sherman and General Hood called a ten-day truce in
mid-September. What was the purpose of this truce?

A. *Sherman had ordered the evacuation of Atlanta by all re-*
maining civilians. They protested angrily, but Sherman re-
plied in a letter, "War is a cruelty and you cannot refine it."
He went on to say—showing another side of his complex
personality—"But, my dear sirs, when peace does come,
you may call on me for any thing. Then I will share with you
the last cracker, and watch with you to shield your homes
and families against danger from any quarter."

Q. Who withdrew as a presidential candidate on September 17?

A. *John C. Frémont, the Radical Democratic candidate, who ultimately decided Lincoln was better than McClellan. He didn't like either man, but was afraid that the vacillating McClellan might allow slavery to survive as a condition of peace.*

Q. Who wrote the following words in connection with Sherman's order that all civilians evacuate Atlanta?

"You come into our country with your army, avowedly for the purpose of subjugating free white men, women and children, and not only intend to rule over them, but you make Negroes your allies, and desire to place over us an inferior race, which we have raised from barbarism to its present position, which is the highest ever attained by that race, in any country, in all time."

A. *These words were addressed to General Sherman by General Hood in an exchange of letters initiated by an outraged Hood. His statements give as good an example as you can find of why the Civil War could continue for another seven months, and why in some quarters it is not over yet.*

Q. General Jubal Early had been moving around in the Shenandoah Valley since his strike north to the outskirts of Washington in May. On September 19, Sheridan attacked Early at the Third Battle of Winchester, and thoroughly defeated him, capturing thousands of Confederate prisoners. Why was this victory received with particular joy in the North?

A. *Because for the first time in the war, the Union was in control of much of the Shenandoah Valley, the breadbasket of the Confederacy and the site of so many Union failures. Sheridan pursued Early and thrashed him again at Fisher's Hill on September 22.*

Q. Who wrote to General Grant in early October of 1864 that by the time he had finished, the Shenandoah Valley from "Winchester up to Staunton, ninety-two miles, will have little in it for man or beast"?

A. *General Sheridan, who was carrying out Grant's order to turn the valley into a barren waste. When he wrote, Sheridan had already destroyed "over 2,000 barns filled with wheat, hay, and farming implements; over seventy mills filled with flour and wheat; have driven in front of the army over 4,000 head of stock, and have killed and issued to the troops not less than 3,000 sheep." A fearful revenge was being taken on an area that had given the Union army so many problems during the previous three years. But the main thing Grant wanted to accomplish was to make certain that if the war continued into the next year, the Confederate army would be even more circumscribed by food shortages.*

Q. On October 13, the raider John Mosby, who had come to be called the "Gray Ghost," derailed a Union passenger train near Kearneysville, West Virginia. He and his band forced two federal paymasters to hand over more than $170,000. What else did they do before escaping?

A. *Burned the train. During 1864, the three most famous Confederate raiders, Mosby, Morgan, and Forrest, had more and more often taken to burning not just trains and military supplies, but also towns where the citizens were Union sympathizers. This was one reason why the North would regard the South as being hypocritical when it howled in protest over Sherman's upcoming devastations. While the scale of Sherman's actions would be much greater, especially in South Carolina, there was widespread feeling in the North that the Confederates had themselves gone over the line much earlier.*

Q. On October 19, General Jubal Early mounted a surprise attack on the forces of General Sheridan, which had been encamped at Cedar Creek near Strasburg in northern Virginia. Sheridan himself was not with his forces when the Confederates attacked at dawn. Where was he?

A. *He had gone to Washington on October 16 to confer with General Grant and President Lincoln on future strategy. Initially, the Confederate attack on the nineteenth made serious headway against the totally unprepared Union forces. But then the Confederate forces slacked off. Early would supposedly say afterward, "The Yankees got whipped, and we got scared."*

Q. The Confederates at Cedar Creek were to get considerably more scared before the day was over. Why?

A. *General Sheridan, returning from Washington, heard the noise of the battle from as far away as Winchester, eight miles to the north, and furiously galloped down the pike and joined his men at the front, riding up and down waving his hat and urging his troops to turn and attack the Confederates. This was the kind of action that inevitably passes into legend, especially when followed by a victory, which his troops were able to achieve quite easily against a Confederate force of desperately underfed men who had stopped to forage for food among the abandoned Union camps. There would never again be a major battle in the Shenandoah Valley.*

Q. What was made a formal national holiday by President Lincoln in response to the continuing Union victories?

A. *Thanksgiving; the announcement was made on October 20.*

192

Q. The Union command had assumed that they would have no more problems in Missouri, but for a month beginning on September 17, a Confederate cavalry force under command of General Sterling Price had been causing serious problems in the state. How many separate Union forces were brought into play to put down Price's incursions?

A. *There were three. One approached from Kansas under General Samuel Curtis, the commander of that department, while General Alfred Pleasonton—who had had a very checkered career—moved in with his cavalry and General A. J. Smith came up from the south. For once, a pincer movement of this kind worked for the North, and at Westport, Missouri, General Price was defeated. There would be no more major problems in Missouri.*

Q. On October 31, 1864, a western territory became the nation's thirty-sixth state, just in time to deliver its three electoral votes to President Lincoln on November 8. Name the new state.

A. *Nevada; its two more-eastern neighbors, Utah and Colorado, would not be admitted until 1896 and 1876, respectively.*

Q. There were only three participating states that Lincoln did not carry on November 8, 1864. Of the following four states, which one *did* he carry?

    a. Delaware
    b. Maryland
    c. New Jersey
    d. Kentucky

A. *He carried Maryland but not the other three. Lincoln got 55 percent of the popular vote, and garnered 212 electoral votes to McClellan's 21.*

The Civil War Quiz Book

Q. How did the vote for president divide among the Union troops in the field, given this contest between Lincoln and the once-beloved General McClellan?

    a. McClellan 42 percent to Lincoln 58 percent
    b. McClellan 35 percent to Lincoln 66 percent
    c. McClellan 30 percent to Lincoln 70 percent

A. *The answer is* b, *which was remarkable considering Mc-Clellan's former standing among the troops.*

Q. In early November, the Confederate troops of General Hood and the Union troops of General Sherman were streaming past one another in opposite directions. Hood was invading Tennessee while Grant was preparing his "march to the sea." What was Hood's motive for invading Tennessee?

A. *It was his hope to draw Sherman into a contest in that state, but Sherman refused to take the bait, believing that General Thomas and his Army of the Cumberland, now in and around Nashville, could take care of any threat from Hood.*

Q. Why did Sherman divide his army as he began his famous "march to the sea"?

A. *In his own words: "The march from Atlanta began on the morning of November 15th, the right wing and cavalry following the railroad southeast toward Jonesboro and General Slocum with the Twentieth Corps leading off to the east by Decatur and Stone Mountain, toward Madison. These were divergent lines, designed to threaten both Macon and Augusta at the same time, so as to prevent a concentration at our intended destination, Milledgeville, the capital of Georgia, distant southeast about one hundred miles. The time allowed each column for reaching Milledgeville was seven days."*

Q. As Sherman's forces approached Milledgeville, the legislature and Governor Joseph Brown fled the city. Which of the following did he *not* take with him, packed into railway cars, from the governor's mansion?

   a.   The carpets, curtains, and furnishings
   b.   The cabbages and other stored vegetables
   c.   Muskets, ammunition, and the public archives

A. *The answer is c. Brown was a controversial figure, originally pro-Union but extremely strong on states' rights issues—so strong that he was constantly at angry odds with Jefferson Davis because Brown refused to abide by orders from Richmond.*

Q. On November 29, General Hood had his troops positioned to attack the badly placed Army of the Ohio under General John Schofield at Spring Hill, Tennessee. What time did the attack begin the next day?

A. *It never took place. In one of the great strategic retreats of the war, Schofield managed to march his entire army to safety in the course of the night, within shouting distance of the Confederates. The Confederates did pursue Schofield but were defeated at Franklin, where Schofield had successfully entrenched his troops.*

Q. By December 10, Sherman had reached his intended destination of Savannah. Why did he decide to besiege the city instead of attacking it directly?

A. *Because General Hardee (who had written the "book" on tactics) had flooded the rice fields around Savannah, leaving only a few narrow strips over which it would be possible to attack.*

The Civil War Quiz Book

Q. On December 15 and 16 General Thomas attacked Hood's Confederate forces at Nashville, Tennessee, and routed the Southern troops. What would have happened if Thomas had not attacked that day?

A. *General Grant would have replaced him. He had already given such an order once, only to rescind it upon receipt of a message from Thomas that promised an attack on the tenth. By the time he did attack on December 15, Thomas was brilliantly organized, and the Confederates never really had a chance. The struggle in Tennessee was now essentially over.*

Q. On December 22, General Sherman presented Lincoln with what he called "a Christmas gift." What was it?

A. *The city of Savannah. The siege had worked in short order and Hardee had withdrawn his troops.*

Q. Name the "political" general who attempted to capture Fort Fisher at Wilmington, North Carolina, and failed dismally.

A. *General Benjamin Butler. With this additional failure, even Butler's great political influence in the North could not save him. To General Grant's great relief, a newly reelected Lincoln finally felt in a position to get rid of the bumbling Butler.*

Part Six
1865

Q. A new constitutional amendment had been passed by the U.S. Senate the previous year, but it had not managed to garner the necessary two-thirds vote in the House of Representatives. In January, Republican supporters of the amendment started to try to persuade some uncertain Democrats to change their votes. What did the amendment call for?

A. *The proposed Thirteenth Amendment abolished slavery, a complete turnaround from the original Thirteenth Amendment of 1860, which had guaranteed slavery. Although the original amendment had passed Congress, it had never been voted on by the states because of the outbreak of the war. Lincoln was determined to get the new amendment through as quickly as possible. Enough Republicans had defeated Democrats in the House so that the next Congress could have passed it with no problem. But the Thirty-ninth Congress would not be duly elected until March 5, and was not scheduled to convene until December. Lincoln was prepared to call a special session, but felt that a bipartisan passage of the amendment by the lame-duck Thirty-eighth Congress would send a much stronger signal.*

Q. On January 13, another attempt to take Fort Fisher in North Carolina got under way as Admiral Porter began a bombardment from the sea to soften up the defenses for a land attack by General Alfred Howe Terry. On January 15, he succeeded in capturing the fort. To what was this success ascribed?

A.   *Even at the time there were wags who suggested that it was simply that fact that General Terry was not General Butler, whom he had succeeded. But that is not giving Terry proper credit. He divided his force of 8,000 approximately in half, one half attacking the fort, the other defending against General Bragg, who had come up at the rear. It was a neatly executed operation that brought General Terry the thanks of Congress ten days later.*

Q.   On January 16, the Confederate Senate overwhelmingly passed a resolution calling for General Lee to be named as General-in-Chief and for General Johnston to be reinstated as Commander of the Army of Tennessee. What was really afoot here?

A.   *It was widely felt in the South by this time that Jefferson Davis was exercising too much personal control over military decisions and that only by upgrading Lee could Davis be controlled. It should be remembered that Davis had not wanted to be the Confederacy's president but its General-in-Chief. In many ways he had taken on that military position, but now he would have to give way. Lee was reluctant to accept, but Davis persuaded him three days later.*

Q.   As January came to a close, Sherman was marching north. His ultimate goal was Goldsboro, North Carolina. But as a diversionary tactic he sent part of his army in the direction of what coastal city?

A.   *Charleston, South Carolina, where Fort Sumter was still in Confederate hands. Sherman really intended to take the in-*

land capital of South Carolina, Columbia, which was on a fairly direct route to Goldsboro.

Q. With whom did President Lincoln and Secretary of State Seward meet aboard the presidential steamship, *River Queen,* off Hampton Roads, Virginia, on February 3, 1865?

A. *Confederate Vice-President Alexander Stephens, the Confederate Senate president pro tempore, Robert Hunter, and the assistant secretary of war for the Confederacy, John A. Campbell, who as a Supreme Court justice had concurred with the Chief Justice in the fateful Dred Scott decision. This Hampton Roads Conference had been brought about as a result of Lincoln's willingness to allow various Northern figures, but particularly Francis P. Blair of Maryland, to approach Jefferson Davis with "peace feelers." The Hampton Roads Conference got nowhere—nor had Lincoln expected it to—but he had felt that it was time to at least begin to talk, if only to make clear that the abolition of slavery and reentry into the Union were the inevitable price of peace.*

Q. On February 5, General Grant ordered some of his troops to move farther to the west of Petersburg in order to cut off another supply route into that city. He had been doing this for six months, sometimes successfully, sometimes not. But by the time this latest extension of the line was completed— and held against a Confederate counterattack the next day—the forces of General Lee were strung out along an increasingly thinly defended perimeter around Petersburg. How long was the Confederate line at this point?

a. 29 miles
b. 39 miles
c. 53 miles

A. *The answer is c, which verged on the untenable. It was only a matter of time before Grant would be able to break through.*

Q. Three state legislatures voted on the adoption of the Thirteenth Amendment on February 8: Delaware, Kansas, and Maine. It passed in two states. In which of the three did it fail to get the necessary two-thirds majority?

A. *Delaware, which had always had more Southern sympathizers than most of the Union states. Kansas, of course, had become a state in 1861 by adopting a constitution that abolished slavery.*

Q. Did General Beauregard or General Wade Hampton, the cavalry commander, attempt to stop General Sherman from entering Columbia, the state capital of South Carolina, on February 1?

A. *No. Both knew that stopping Sherman was impossible. Hampton, who was one of the richest landowners in the South, had a great mansion in Columbia, which he was forced to evacuate. During the night of February 17–18, as fires raged out of control in Columbia, his home was one of those destroyed. Sherman stated immediately that the fires spread from cotton that fleeing Confederates had set on fire, and he and his men helped citizens of Columbia in trying to put out the fires—a fact that many Southerners still refuse to accept.*

Q. Although Sherman officially ordered only the burning of warehouses, railroad depots, and other facilities that were of military significance, the progress of his march through South Carolina was marked by much destruction of homes and private property. Much of this was carried out by stragglers and camp followers, but there is little question that some Union troops were out of control during this period and that Sherman did not do as much as he might have to control them. Why was it that so much destruction of private property took place in South Carolina but almost completely stopped once the Union army entered North Carolina in mid-March?

A. *South Carolina, the most militant of all the Confederate States concerning slavery and the first to secede from the Union, was widely seen in the North as the principal fomenter of the Civil War. Thus there is no doubt that the destruction of personal property in the state was often carried out in a spirit of revenge. The debate over what happened as Sherman moved through South Carolina—and bitter arguments can still erupt even today—goes to the heart of the very different ways in which North and South viewed the Civil War from the start.*

Q. What was attached to an oar and a boathook and placed atop Fort Sumter on February 18, 1865?

A. *The Union flag was hung from this temporary staff as the North regained possession of Fort Sumter for the first time since the beginning of the war. Once Sherman had captured Columbia, and his army was between Charleston and any Confederate reinforcements, General Hardee was forced to abandon Charleston and Fort Sumter, which had now been bombarded from the sea for twenty months.*

Q. On February 20, the Confederate House passed a bill authorizing something that the Senate voted to postpone the next day. What was it?

A. *Arming slaves and using them as soldiers.*

Q. Secretary of the Treasury Salmon P. Chase, who had caused Lincoln problems throughout the war, had submitted his resignation numerous times. To his surprise, Lincoln had finally accepted it on June 30 of the previous year. But what was Chase doing on March 4, 1865?

A. *As the new Chief Justice of the Supreme Court, he was administering the oath of Office to Abraham Lincoln as he was sworn in for his second term as president of the United States on the steps of the Capitol, the dome of which was finally nearing completion. By naming Chase as Chief Justice, Lincoln had removed a rival from the political scene and at the same time gained an ally in some of the more controversial areas of his plans for Reconstruction.*

Q. Lincoln's second inaugural address contained what is probably the second most famous sentence he ever uttered, after the opening of the Gettysburg Address. What were the first four words of that sentence in the second inaugural address?

A. *"With Malice toward none . . ."*

Q. On March 8, Confederate General Braxton Bragg attacked a Union force under the command of General Jacob Cox near Kinston, North Carolina. What was Bragg trying to prevent?

A. *His goal was to turn the Union forces back and stop them from linking up with General Sherman's troops, which had crossed into North Carolina and were moving toward Fayetteville in the south-central portion of the state. Fighting went on for three days around Kinston, but Bragg was unable to dislodge the Union force.*

Q. The Confederate Senate had delayed passage of the bill calling for the recruitment of slaves as soldiers, arguing over whether or not such soldiers should be freed upon joining up. How did they settle this debate?

A. *By leaving the question up to each individual state. The bill was passed and signed by Jefferson Davis on March 13.*

Q. As General Cox's troops continued westward through North Carolina, what were they doing to help establish a new supply line to the North Carolina coast?

A. *They repaired the rail lines as they went.*

Q. Sherman sent the left wing of his army, under General Henry Slocum, straight north, as though Raleigh and not Goldsboro to the east were the ultimate objective. Why did this action prove to be a problem?

A. *General Johnston, whom Lee had called out of retirement, had amassed 20,000 troops along this line and attacked Slocum near Bentonville on March 19. This forced Sherman to bring the rest of his army to the rescue. By the night of March 21, Johnston was withdrawing to Smithfield, and Sherman returned to his march to Goldsboro, which was reached on March 23. Here he joined forces with General Schofield's troops, which had arrived from the North Carolina coast.*

Q. Who arrived at City Point, Virginia, with his wife and son on March 25?

A. *President Lincoln, on a visit to the Army of the Potomac headquarters on the James River. The Confederates had, that very morning, made an assault on Fort Stedman, held by the Union, in an attempt to force Grant to shorten the length of his line at Petersburg. By the end of the day, however, the attack had been turned back. Lincoln decided to stay on, expecting the end to come soon.*

Q. On March 31, General Sheridan and his cavalry, which had arrived at Petersburg four days earlier, joined General Warren in an attack on Confederates under General Pickett to the southwest of Petersburg. The Confederate line held, but Pickett then fell back to another position at Five Forks that night. Why?

A. *Because he felt that the Union force was too large to be resisted further. Although admonished by Lee not to give up his position at Five Forks no matter what, Pickett was overwhelmed by Sheridan the following day.*

Q. On Sunday, April 2, Jefferson Davis got a message as he was attending church. What was the message and whom was it from?

A. *The message advised him to evacuate Richmond because Petersburg could no longer be held; it came from General Lee, who had issued an early warning about the situation on March 26. Davis and much of his Cabinet took a special train the night of April 2 southwest to Danville, Virginia, on the North Carolina border.*

Q. Also on April 2, Union cavalry under General James H. Wilson took Selma, Alabama, from the troops of General Nathan Bedford Forrest, who was almost captured. Why had this raid against Selma been regarded as important?

A. *Aside from Richmond itself, Selma was one of the last industrial towns not already in Union hands. That same night, the industrial capacity of Richmond itself was destroyed as Confederate troops burned anything of military value. The flames get out of hand and large sections of the Confederate capital were gutted.*

Q. Also on the night of April 2, Lee began to move his troops out of Petersburg. Did all the Confederate troops withdraw at once?

A. *No. Forces under command of General James Longstreet and General John B. Gordon remained to slow down any Union pursuit. In the fighting the next day, General A. P. Hill, who had fought so valiantly at Antietam and Fredricksburg, was killed. He had suffered from an unknown illness since the Battle of Gettysburg, and had never been the same.*

Q. Why was Admiral David Porter so nervous about sailing up the James River to the fallen and occupied city of Richmond on April 4?

A. *His main passenger was President Lincoln, and Porter was fearful that some remaining Confederate sharpshooter might try to kill Lincoln as he walked the streets of burnt-out Richmond. But Lincoln was surrounded by so many hundreds of joyous blacks, slaves no more, that he might as well have been protected by an entire regiment instead of only ten sailors. The President made a famous remark that day when a black man fell to his knees at Lincoln's feet. "Don't kneel to me," he said. "That is not right. You must kneel to God only, and thank him for the liberty you will enjoy hereafter."*

Q. What quality for which he was famous helped General Sheridan get into a position on April 7 that made the surrender of Lee inevitable?

A. *Speed. Sheridan managed to get his cavalry and two divisions of infantry to the southwest of Lee and was at Appomattox Court House to block Lee's line of retreat from Meade's forces coming up behind him. Until he found himself almost surrounded near Appomattox on April 9, Lee had planned to continue fighting, despite an exchange with Grant by messenger concerning possible peace terms two days earlier.*

Q. In the early afternoon of April 9, Lee and Grant met at a farmhouse near Appomattox to discuss the terms of surrender. Why was the owner of this house, Wilmer McLean, absolutely stunned at what was occurring in his parlor?

A. *It was McLean whose farm had been totally destroyed at the battle of Gettysburg—beginning with an artillery shell that had landed in his dining room. He had packed up and moved to this out-of-the-way village in the hope that the war would never again disrupt his day-to-day life.*

Q. The terms of surrender were essentially those that had been formulated by Grant at Vicksburg—all munitions would be surrendered, except sidearms, which were often the personal property of soldiers, and the troops were to return home on "parole" until a Union prisoner was exchanged. It was understood on both sides, however, that these Confederate soldiers would never be returning to battle. Lee requested and Grant acceded to an additional provision concerning another sort of personal property. What was this provision?

A. *The Confederate officers and troops would be allowed to return home with any horse or mule that they claimed to own. Grant, in his own handwriting, noted that they should take the "animals home with them to work their little farms."*

Q. Returning to his troops, General Lee told them, "Go to your homes and resume your occupations. Obey the laws and become as good citizens as you were soldiers." From what vantage point did Lee speak these words?

A. *Astride his beloved old gray horse, Traveller, whom he had ridden since the beginning of the war.*

Q. The celebrations throughout the North on April 10, 1865, were tumultuous. Crowds at the White House asked Lincoln for a speech, but he demurred, saying that he would make one the next day. That speech was careful, but it included a remark concerning the possibility of giving the vote to black soldiers as well as to what were called "intelligent"—meaning literate—blacks. This caused one man listening to the speech to say to a companion, "That means nigger citizenship." Who spoke these words?

A. *John Wilkes Booth, who added, "Now, by God, I'll put him through. This is the last speech he will ever make."*

Q. On April 12, the formal surrender of Lee's Army of Northern Virginia took place at Appomattox Court House, with General Joshua Chamberlain representing Grant and General John B. Gordon representing Lee. What did General Chamberlain call out that astonished, and deeply affected, General Gordon?

A. *Chamberlain gave the order to "Carry arms," the salute of honor, and as the Union troops followed the order, Gordon called out for his own dejected troops to follow suit. The end thus came with more dignity and mutual respect than most people on either side would have thought possible.*

Q. What was the name of the play that President Lincoln, his wife, Major Henry Rathbone, and his fiancée, Clara Harris, attended at Ford's Theater on Friday night, April 14?

A. *It was a comedy called* Our American Cousin *by Laura Keene, an English playwright and actress who was also playing the leading role. At about 10:00 P.M., John Wilkes Booth, one of the lesser lights of the great acting family, stepped into Lincoln's box and fired a single shot into the president's head just behind the ear. He then stabbed Major Rathbone and leaped over the box railing to the stage below. In the process he broke his left leg but was still able to escape on a horse he had waiting for him at the stage door. Lincoln would die at 7:22 A.M.*

Q. As Booth was shooting Lincoln, a co-conspirator named Lewis T. Powell, who was using the alias Lewis Payne, broke into the home of Secretary of State William Seward. Seward was in bed recuperating from a serious carriage accident that he had suffered while visiting Richmond with Lincoln on April 5. Powell stabbed Seward several times around the face and neck. What medical device probably saved Seward's life?

A. *The neck brace he was wearing prevented Powell from severing the jugular vein. Powell was pulled off by Seward's son and a male nurse, but he was a very powerfully built man and managed to escape.*

Q. Booth was eventually cornered in a tobacco barn near Port Royal, Virginia. His co-conspirator David E. Herold, who had traveled with Booth from Washington, came out of the barn and gave himself up, but Booth refused. The barn was set on fire and then a shot rang out that killed Booth, but it has never been established whether he shot himself or was killed by a bullet fired by one of the cavalry detachment that cornered him. As the rest of the conspirators were captured, it became clear that earlier in the year Booth had planned to kidnap Lincoln. What had he intended to do with him?

A. *Take him to Richmond and hold him hostage until all Confederate prisoners were released by the North. There were eight conspirators charged in the case, and all were convicted at a rather high-handed military trial presided over by General Lew Wallace. Four of the conspirators, including Mrs. Mary Surratt, who had kept the boardinghouse where Booth lodged, were hanged on July 7, but there have always been questions about her guilt. Questions were also raised about the conviction of Dr. Samuel Mudd, the retired physician who set Booth's broken leg. Mudd was imprisoned at Dry Tortugas, Florida, but was pardoned by President Johnson in 1867 after the doctor performed heroically during an outbreak of yellow fever at the prison.*

Q. On April 21, President Lincoln's casket was taken from the Capitol where it had been on view, and put aboard a special funeral train that was to carry Lincoln home to Springfield, Illinois, for burial. The train made many stops along the way so that respects could be paid by the people to the fallen president. How long did it take for the train to reach its final destination?

A. *It took thirteen days. The casket was put on view in state capitols or other central buildings in Baltimore, Harrisburg, Philadelphia, New York, Albany, Buffalo, Cleveland, Columbus, and finally Springfield. During those thirteen days, the casket, or the slow sad passing of the funeral train, were viewed by an estimated seven million people.*

Q. On April 26, General Johnston surrendered his army of 30,000 to General Sherman. An earlier peace agreement had been reached between the two men, but had been rejected by President Andrew Johnson. Why?

A. *Johnson felt the agreement was too broad and insisted upon terms that were nearly the same as those Lee had accepted. Sherman was criticized for overstepping his role.*

Q. On May 10, Jefferson Davis and his wife were captured by Union cavalry near Irwinville, Georgia. What was done with Davis?

A. *He was taken to Richmond and confined to a cell at Fort Monroe in chains. Charged with treason, but never brought to trial, he was finally released on bail two years later.*

Q. With the surrender of all Confederate troops west of the Mississippi on May 26, the Civil War came to an end. Were there any Confederate troops that did not surrender?

A. *Yes. Cavalry leader General Joseph Shelby and some of his troops went to Mexico. But even he eventually returned to Missouri, where he had business interests.*

Q. The only soldier to be awarded the Congressional Medal of Honor during the Civil War was killed in the massacre at the Little Big Horn in 1876. Name him.

A. *Thomas Ward Custer, the younger brother of General George Custer. Still only nineteen, in the last days of the war he captured the rebel flag in two engagements within three days, on April 3 and April 6. In the latter battle of Sayler's Creek, he was wounded in the face but continued to fight. His older brother had to place him under military arrest and have him forcibly removed from the field to get medical attention.*

Q. Which of the following states provided the largest number of Union soldiers and which the least: Ohio, New York, Illinois, Rhode Island, Tennessee?

A. *New York provided the most, 448,850. Rhode Island sent the least, 23,236, although that was a considerable number given the size of the state. The deeply divided state of Tennessee sent almost 10,000 more than Rhode Island to support the Union cause.*

Q. How many more Confederate soldiers died as prisoners of war than did Union soldiers?

    a. 4
    b. 400
    c. 4,000

A. *The answer is* a. *The loss for the Confederacy was 30,156, to 30,152 for the Union. These are official figures but they have often been questioned.*

Q. How many more Union soldiers died in the Civil War than Confederate soldiers?

    a. 60,000
    b. 100,000
    c. 120,000

A. *The answer is* b, *with about 360,000 Union dead. Civilian casualties were certainly much greater in the South, however.*

Q. How many poems did Walt Whitman write lamenting the death of Lincoln?

A. *There were four. Two were minor works that were quickly forgotten. The third, "O Captain! My Captain!," was an instant and huge success. The fourth poem, long and in blank verse, was largely ignored for more than half a century. It was not until the 1920s that "When Lilacs Last in the Dooryard Bloom'd" was recognized as Whitman's master-*

piece and the greatest elegy ever written by an American. It begins with these three lines:

When lilacs last in the dooryard bloom'd,
And the great star early droop'd in the western sky in the night,
I mourn'd—and yet shall mourn with ever-returning spring.

Bibliography

Abdill, George B. *Civil War Railroads*. New York: Bonanza Books, 1961.

Anders, Curt. *Fighting Confederates*. New York: Dorset Press, 1968.

Atlantic Monthly, The, Vols. VIII–XVI. Boston: Ticknor and Fields, 1861–1865.

Boatner, Mark M., III. *The Civil War Dictionary*. New York: David McKay, 1959.

Bowman, John S., ed. *The Civil War Day by Day*. Greenwich, Conn.: Dorset Press, 1990.

Catton, Bruce. *The Coming Fury*. Garden City, N.Y.: Doubleday and Co., Inc., 1961.

———. *Gettysburg: The Final Fury*. Garden City, N.Y.: Doubleday and Co., Inc., 1974.

———. *Never Call Retreat*. Garden City, N.Y.: Doubleday and Co., Inc., 1965.

———. *A Stillness at Appomattox*. Garden City, N.Y.: Doubleday and Co., Inc., 1954.

Bibliography

————. *Terrible Swift Sword.* Garden City, N.Y.: Doubleday and Co., Inc., 1963.

Commager, Henry Steele. *Documents of American History.* New York: Appleton-Century-Crofts, 1958.

Coulter, E. Merton. *The Confederate States of America, 1861–1865.* Baton Rouge: Louisiana State University Press, 1950.

Craven, Avery. *The Coming of the Civil War.* New York: Charles Scribner's Sons, 1942.

Cullen, Joseph P. *The Peninsula Campaign.* Harrisburg, Pa.: Stackpole Books, 1973.

Davis, Burke. *The Civil War: Strange and Fascinating Facts.* New York: Fairfax Press, 1982.

————. *The Long Surrender.* New York: Vintage Books, 1989.

————. *Sherman's March.* New York: Vintage Books, 1980.

————. *They Called Him Stonewall.* New York: Rinehart & Company, 1954.

Foner, Eric. *Free Soil, Free Labor, Free Men.* New York: Oxford University Press, 1970.

Foote, Shelby. *The Civil War: A Narrative.* 3 Vols. New York: Random House, 1958, 1963, 1974.

Freeman, Douglas Southall. *Lee's Lieutenants.* 3 Vols. New York: Charles Scribner's Sons, 1940–46.

Genovese, Eugene D. *Roll, Jordan, Roll.* New York: Random House, 1974.

Harwell, Richard B. *The Confederate Reader.* New York: Dover Publications, 1984.

Hicks, Roger W., and Frances E. Schultz. *Battlefields of the Civil War.* Topsfield, Mass.: Salem House, 1989.

Horan, James D. *Mathew Brady.* New York: Bonanaza Books, 1955.

Howarth, Stephen. *To Shining Sea: A History of the United States Navy.* New York: Random House, 1991.

Johnson, Rossiter. *Campfires and Battlefields.* New York: Civil War Press, 1967.

Ketchum, Richard M., ed. *The American Heritage Picture*

Bibliography

History of the Civil War, Vol. II. Garden City, N.Y.: Doubleday and Co., Inc., 1960.

Long, E. B., and Barbara Long. *The Civil War Day by Day.* Garden City, N.Y.: Doubleday and Co., Inc., 1971.

Lossing, Benson J. *Mathew Brady's Illustrated History of the Civil War.* New York: The Fairfax Press, facsimile of 1912 edition.

McPherson, James M. *Battle Cry of Freedom.* New York: Oxford University Press, 1988.

Malone, Dumas, and Basil Rauch. *Empire for Liberty,* Vol. I. New York: Appleton-Century-Crofts, 1960.

Martin, David G. *The Shiloh Campaign.* New York: The Fairfax Press, 1987.

Milligan, John D. *Gunboats Down the Mississippi.* Annapolis, Md.: U.S. Naval Institute, 1965.

Mitchell, Joseph B. *Decisive Battles of the Civil War.* New York: G. P. Putnam's Sons, 1955.

Moat, Louis Shepheard, ed. *Frank Leslie's Illustrated Famous Leaders and Battle Scenes of the Civil War.* New York: Mrs. Frank Leslie, Publisher, 1896.

Moehring, Eugene P., and Arleen Keylin, eds. *The Civil War Extra.* New York: Arno Press, 1975.

Oates, Stephen B. *With Malice Toward None.* New York: Harper and Row, 1977.

O'Connor, Thomas H. *The Disunited States.* New York: Harper and Row, 1978.

Roller, David C., and Robert W. Twyman, eds. *The Encyclopedia of Southern History.* Baton Rouge: Louisiana State University Press, 1979.

ROTC Manual No. 145-20. *American Military History.* Washington, D.C.: Department of the Army, 1956.

Sherman, William T. *Marching Through Georgia,* ed. Mills Lane. New York: Arno Press, 1978.

Sifakis, Stewart. *Who Was Who in the Civil War.* New York: Facts on File, 1988.

Stackpole, Edward J. *They Met at Gettysburg.* Harrisburg, Pa.: Eagle Books, 1956.

Bibliography

Stampp, Kenneth M., ed. *The Causes of the Civil War*. Englewood Cliffs, N.J.: Prentice-Hall, 1974.

Steere, Edward. *The Wilderness Campaign*. Harrisburg, Pa.: The Stockpole Company, 1960.

Stern, Philip Van Doren. *Secret Missions of the Civil War*. New York: Bonanza, 1990.

Stimson, Henry L. *Atlas to Accompany the Official Records of the Union and Confederate Armies*. Washington, D.C.: The War Department, n.d.

Swisher, Carl Brent. *American Constitutional Development*. Boston: Houghton Mifflin, 1954.

Syndor, Charles S. *The Development of Southern Sectionalism, 1819–1848*. Baton Rouge: Louisiana State University Press, 1948.

Wert, Jeffry D. *From Winchester to Cedar Creek*. New York: Touchstone, 1987.

Wheeler, Richard. *Sword over Richmond*. New York: Harper and Row, 1986.

Whitman, Walt. *Selected Poems*. New York: Dover Publications, Inc., 1991.

Williams, T. Harry. *Lincoln and His Generals*. New York: Knopf, 1952.

Wilson, Woodrow. *Division and Reunion*. New York: Longmans, Green and Co., 1921.